I0124448

Open access edition supported by the National Endowment for the Humanities /
Andrew W. Mellon Foundation Humanities Open Book Program.

© 2019 Johns Hopkins University Press
Published 2019

Johns Hopkins University Press
2715 North Charles Street
Baltimore, Maryland 21218-4363
www.press.jhu.edu

ISBN-13: 978-1-4214-3469-8 (open access)
ISBN-10: 1-4214-3469-5 (open access)

ISBN-13: 978-1-4214-3467-4 (pbk. : alk. paper)
ISBN-10: 1-4214-3467-9 (pbk. : alk. paper)

ISBN-13: 978-1-4214-3468-1 (electronic)
ISBN-10: 1-4214-3468-7 (electronic)

This page supersedes the copyright page included in the original publication of this work.

LEOPOLD III

AND THE BELGIAN ROYAL QUESTION

LEOPOLD III
AND
THE BELGIAN
ROYAL QUESTION

BY

E. RAMÓN ARANGO

The Johns Hopkins Press   Baltimore

A prince is further esteemed when he is a true friend or a true enemy, when, that is, he declares himself without reserve in favor of some one or against another. This policy is always more useful than remaining neutral. For if two neighboring powers come to blows, they are either such that if one wins, you will have to fear the victor, or else not. In either of these two cases it will be better for you to declare yourself openly and make war, because in the first case if you do not declare yourself, you will fall a prey to the victor, to the pleasure and satisfaction of the one who has been defeated, and you will have no reason nor anything to defend you and nobody to receive you. For, whoever wins will not desire friends whom he suspects and who do not help him when in trouble, and whoever loses will not receive you as you did not take up arms to venture yourself in his cause.

MACHIAVELLI
THE PRINCE

TO

CAROLINE AND ERGASTO ARANGO

AND

ALFRED DIAMANT

PREFACE

I am grateful to Professors Manning Dauer and Frederick Hartmann, of the University of Florida, and particularly to Professor Alfred Diamant, of Haverford College.

I find myself in debt to many Belgians whose suggestions and insights sharpened my understanding of the royal question. I hope that they will feel that I have helped to clarify a part of their history and politics which has too long been in the shadow of doubt and surmise.

I do not know Flemish; consequently, there are no Flemish sources in the bibliography. I do not believe, however, that this omission has prejudiced my study. Had I an anti-Leopold bias, it could be attributed to a failure to use Flemish materials, which are overwhelmingly pro-Leopold. But I am neither pro-Leopold nor anti-Leopold, and when I question his behavior I do not do so from that point of view condemned by the Walloons and defended by the Flemings. Moreover, the position of most Flemings was the same as that of the pro-Leopold Social Christian party, the Catholic party, while the position of most anti-Leopold Flemings followed either the Socialist or Liberal line. Source material concerning these parties was available in both Flemish and French. Furthermore, all official governmental publications, including the transcriptions of the parliamentary debates, appear in both languages, as do the publications of the trade unions and other nation-wide organizations. Finally, the major works about Belgian history and politics, as well as the articles in most learned journals, are written in French.

All the French sources were translated by me, and I am responsible for their accuracy.

CONTENTS

CHAPTER 4

THE ROYAL QUESTION TAKES SHAPE

CHAPTER 5

THE GOVERNMENT'S CASE AGAINST LEOPOLD

CHAPTER 6

LEOPOLD'S DEFENSE: THE REPORT
OF THE COMMISSION OF INFORMATION

CHAPTER 7

THE END OF THE ROYAL QUESTION

CHAPTER 8

LIST OF TABLES

LEOPOLD III

AND THE BELGIAN ROYAL QUESTION

INTRODUCTION

On may 10, 1940, the Germans invaded Belgium. At the end of fifteen days, when defeat appeared certain, the Belgian government fled into exile so that it might carry on the war from France and later from England. Contrary to the pleadings and advice of his ministers, the Belgian king, Leopold III, chose to stay in Belgium and share the fate of his army and his subjects. Three days later, on May 28, Leopold, acting in his capacity as commander-in-chief of the armed forces, capitulated to the enemy and was taken prisoner. He remained a captive until May, 1945. The separation of King and Cabinet on May 25, 1940, marked the beginning of what the Belgians call the royal question, which came to an end on August 1, 1950, when Leopold III abdicated in favor of his son, Prince Baudouin.

Essentially the royal question is the final episode in a long-developing dispute over conflicting interpretations of monarchical power under the Constitution. The Constitution divides power generously between the king and Parliament; yet as Belgian political life evolved from 1830 until 1940, particularly with the growth of political parties and responsible party government, power came to lie increasingly in Parliament. Belgium's first two monarchs, Leopold I and Leopold II, resisted this evolution and used their full constitutional power. The third king, Albert, who reigned from 1909 until 1934, either because of his personality or because he understood the political changes taking place, acquiesced in the pre-eminence of the legislature. He ruled, however, during a period of relative stability and died before the events of the

1

second half of the 1930's could test his continued forbearance. He was succeeded by his son, thirty-three-year-old Leopold III. The mid-1930's were an inauspicious time to come to the throne. Emile Cammaerts wrote that one could rummage in vain through history to find a young constitutional monarch confronted with more pressing and anxious problems from the very first days of his reign. The world depression and the economic policies of France and Germany threatened Belgium with financial ruin. The military strength of Nazi Germany was growing to frightening proportions while Belgium's historic allies, England and France, did nothing to stop it.

In Belgium, the parliamentary process was unable to handle the crisis situations. Fascist parties in both Flanders and Wallonia menaced national stability, while divisions within the major parties hampered the normal parliamentary process. Cabinets followed one another with dramatic regularity, and King Leopold was forced to act in order to maintain governmental continuity. As a consequence, he was compelled to make decisions that identified him with specific policies. In 1935, attempting to rescue Belgium from economic collapse, Leopold called Paul Van Zeeland from outside Parliament to head a tripartite national government.[1] Van Zeeland, identified with Leopold, was granted extraordinary power in economic affairs. In 1936, after Hitler had marched into the Rhineland, it was Leopold who called for a new Belgian foreign policy. He made his proposal privately at a meeting of the Council of Ministers, but the members of the Cabinet requested that the proposal be made public. The King agreed, and the Government assumed responsibility, but Leopold and neutrality became synonymous. The Belgians thus identified

[1] Paul Van Zeeland, prior to entering the government, had been a vice-governor of the *Banque Nationale*. He was considered one of Belgium's great economists and had taught at the Catholic University of Louvain. He had been a minister without portfolio in the de Broqueville Cabinet created in June, 1934, but resigned when the Cabinet fell in November, 1934, and returned to his position as vice-governor of the *Banque Nationale*.

their sovereign personally with the two most important events of the immediate prewar years, a situation which went counter to the then current concept of the position of a constitutional monarch. More significantly, Leopold identified himself with these policies and what he considered to be the "greater good of Belgium."

What took place during the brief fighting war, May 10 to 28, 1940, was the last of the series of events which had started in 1935 and 1936. On May 25, 1940, when his ministers advised Leopold to leave Belgium and accompany them into exile, the King had other ideas regarding what he thought would be best for the nation. He chose to stay behind to share the fate of his troops and his people. This decision and the events that resulted from it during the occupation make up the royal question, a constitutional issue containing this paradox: before the war, the Constitution was vague enough to permit a variety of discrepant interpretations regarding the limits of monarchical power. Convention was eroding the personal prerogatives of the sovereign so that constitutionally he had authority that was no longer recognized by current usage. Yet events compelled Leopold to act with full power contrary to evolving custom, and this brought into the open the discrepancy between what Leopold considered to lie within his constitutional authority and the evolving "rules of the game." The separation on May 25, 1940, was the final dramatization of this discrepancy.

After the war, both the Government which had been in exile and King Leopold sought from the Belgian people vindication of their respective decisions. The ministers believed that they had been right to continue the war from beyond the borders of Belgium; the King believed that he had been right to surrender his troops in order to prevent their annihilation by what appeared to be an invincible enemy. Ratification of these decisions and their consequences carried with it, however, endorsement of a particular interpretation of monarchical authority under the Constitution. Can the king make and execute a decision contrary to the advice of responsible ministers? To answer the question affirmatively would vindicate the King. To answer the question negatively would vindicate the Government and relegate the King and his successors to a position of authority comparable to that of other modern constitutional monarchs. The future relationship between Belgian sovereigns and their ministers—in fact, the future of the constitutional monarchy in Belgium, depended upon the outcome of the dispute.

The royal question was more than this, however. No such technical, constitutional issue could have captured and sustained the interest of the people; yet the royal question was the most personal and the most violent public issue ever to occur in Belgian history because it touched the weakest element in Belgian society, its unity. There are two ethnic groups within Belgium, the Flemish and the Walloon. During the years of the debate over the royal question, the Flemish (Flemish-speaking) provinces of the kingdom contained 50.19 per cent of the population (4,272,000), while the Walloon (French-speaking) areas had 34.54 per cent (2,912,000). The Brussels metropolitan region (*l'agglomération bruxelloise*) held the remainder (1,298,000), containing both Flemings and Walloons. But because French is the principal spoken language of Brussels, the region has a predominantly Walloon appearance. In recent years the French-speaking elements of the Brussels area have grown rapidly as Flemish families moving into the "big city" change their daily spoken language to French, thereby adding to the number of French-speaking people in the region.

These groups differ not only in language but also in culture and outlook; one might even say they differ in religion. The majority of Belgians is considered to be Catholic, but the Flemings are devout, loyal, and conservative, while the Walloons are often lukewarm and anticlerical, influenced strongly by the intellectual currents coming from France. The Flemings and the Walloons exist in the artificial entity called Belgium, a political unit created by international design in 1815, and they react centrifugally in relation to national unity. These efferent forces have shaped the country's history and have caused serious strain on national cohesion even in times of peace; in times of war the forces react even more violently. The clash is acute owing primarily to the extraordinary attachment of Wallonia to France. The pro-German sympathy of Flanders is much less intense in comparison and often appears to be a reaction against Walloon attraction to France rather than a deep-seated emotion in itself. The Walloon is passionately devoted to France and is often prouder of his adopted French culture than of his Belgian birth. During wartime this devotion was magnified, and the average Walloon thought that anyone who was not pro-French was automatically pro-German.

The behavior of King Leopold III during the German occupation could not be called pro-French or even pro-Allied. As a result of his policy, Leopold brought down upon himself the animosity and eventually the hatred not only of the Walloons but also of most of the citizens of Brussels. Those who would not venture to say that Leopold had collaborated were convinced that he had believed that the Germans would be victorious and had courted their favor, behavior which Leopold's enemies considered only slightly less repugnant than collaboration. More dispassionate observers think that King Leopold neither collaborated nor believed in a German victory, but he did not discount the possibility. If the Germans should be victorious Leopold hoped to gain the maximum advantage for Belgium, and his behavior during the occupation was designed to accommodate himself to this eventuality. One can imagine that Leopold reasoned like this: the Belgian government fights with the Allies while the King is a prisoner of the Germans. He will do nothing to aid the aggressor, but he will do nothing to offend him. Irrespective of who is the victor, that victor will have a Belgian friend, or, in the case of Leopold, if not a friend, at least not an avowed enemy. This was the policy of *attentisme*, "wait and see," "wait and profit."

Whether it was called collaboration, *attentisme*, or what Victor Larock described as "supple accommodation," the Walloons and the people of Brussels considered Leopold's behavior to be immoral, and after the war they sought through political action to repudiate him. At this point, the two elements of the royal question, i.e., the constitutional and the political, or what the average Belgian would call moral, merged and found their spokesman in the Socialist party. The Socialists in Belgium have been historically opposed to a strong monarchy. In theory, Socialists are republican, but because the monarchy is considered to be essential to Belgian national existence, the Belgian Socialists have always tolerated the monarchy, while at the same time they have fought for the reduction of monarchical power. Therefore, in the constitutional dispute between the King and the Government, the Socialists supported the Government against the King, and because the Socialists are predominantly Walloon, their political or moral opposition to Leopold III strengthened and became a part of the constitutional dispute.

The purpose of this study is to show the monarchy as it existed before the royal question (1935–1940); to present the events that made up the question itself (1940–1944); to describe the battle between the King and the Government as each sought to win the approval of the people (1945–1947); to reveal the solution of the royal question (1949–1950); and finally to speculate on the nature of the monarchy after 1950, on the significance of the ten-year affair on the future relationship between Belgian sovereigns and their governments, and on the relevance of the Belgian experience for an understanding of the role of a constitutional monarch in modern, democratic society.

CHAPTER 1

THE MONARCHY: ITS ORIGINS AND FUNCTIONS

The Nature of the Belgian Monarchy

It has been said that in Belgium the monarchy is as necessary as bread. It is unfortunate that a modern democracy, such as Belgium, should find itself dependent upon a single institution. This reliance makes national life precarious and seems to indicate a flaw in the composition of the body politic. By contrast, in England, as closely as one identifies the Crown with the nation, it would not be fanciful to assume that Britain would continue to exist without her sovereign. The same would be true of Holland and the Scandinavian countries. This is so because the monarchy is today an adornment without which national life would be more complicated, in whose absence readjustment would have to be made, but whose demise would not occasion the collapse of the national state.

Yet, even though not essential to national existence, the British monarchy has survived and flourished. Ernest Barker has said that the secret lies in the monarchy's willingness to change and in its ability to offer stability amid this change:

The continuity of our monarchy inspires us with a sense of the continuity of our national life through a long and storied past. . . . But it is far, very far, from being a merely conservative institution. It does not prevent change. On the contrary, it has helped and fostered change, and it has changed itself in the process. This is the cause of its long survival. It has survived because it has changed and because it has moved with the movement of time. It has survived because our kings, for the last 250 years . . . have been wise enough to forget past pretentions, to learn new lessons, to change their positions with changing time, and to join with the subjects in bringing about change in other institutions.[1]

In Belgium, this was the lesson that Albert I learned but did not teach to his son, Leopold III. The latter's lack of flexibility was in large part responsible for the royal question.

There is yet another factor which has contributed to the success of the British monarchy, a factor more fundamental than the personal willingness of individual monarchs to change with the times. The absence of this element in Belgium accounts significantly for the difficulties suffered by its monarchy. The British sovereign, like the Dutch and the Scandinavian sovereigns, is the embodiment of historical continuity and national self-identification, but he functions in this capacity only because there already exists a tradition common to all of his subjects and because the people, of which he is the reflection, are whole and able to be mirrored in a single, undistorted image. In short, the Crown is the result, not the cause, of consensus and homogeneity, and consequently is not essential to their continuance. This was not always true. Western European monarchies existed historically where these two factors were missing, but those monarchies were powerful institutions with wide discretion and far-reaching influence. It was

[1] Ernest Barker, *Essays on Government* (Oxford: At the Clarendon Press, 1951), pp. 2–3.

the function of the king personally to maintain the unity that would be nonexistent without him. As monarchies evolved, however, and the power of the sovereign was circumscribed, monarchical institutions continued to flourish only in those countries which were or became homogeneous and unified— socially, politically, religiously, and psychologically. The sovereign then lost his active function as a unifier and assumed the passive role as symbol of an established unity, a symbol whose stability is in direct proportion to its dispensability.

In Belgium, the monarchy is indispensable to national unity, a maxim which commands the faith of Catholic, Liberal, and Socialist. It is the king who stands above the provincial conflicts of Wallonia and Flanders, and it is through him alone that the Fleming and the Walloon identifies himself as Belgian. But the Crown violates thereby the two postulates upon which it is claimed a viable constitutional monarchy rests, consensus and homogeneity. It violates them because the Belgian monarchy is not truly constitutional (as is the British after which it was patterned but with which it had little in common except nomenclature). It is a hybrid designed to reconcile two concepts of monarchy, each of which answers a peculiar Belgian need: it is a constitutional monarchy whose sovereign is granted power disproportionate to that of a constitutional monarch in order that he accomplish an authoritative function, the maintenance of national unity. This hybrid creation functions smoothly so long as the elements of national division in which the king is forced to find the common denominator remain quiescent. If the divisive elements do become active, the monarchy continues to operate effectively only so long as the king's power is maintained.

It should be observed that all monarchies have suffered periods of change as a result of which the power of the sovereign was reduced, but for the most part those periods occurred *before* the development of the system of constitutional monarchy and were steps leading to its establishment. Once the system is entrenched, little significant change takes place in the power of the monarch. In other words, in a constitutional monarchy the sovereign occupies an evolved, not an evolving, position.

One finds the most characteristic evidence of this in Great Britain. From the beginning of the modern monarchy, which may be said to date from the first Tudor sovereign in 1485, the history of the British monarchy might be considered as an evolution from personal royal prerogative to what is described today, and has been so described since the reign of George IV, as "the Crown in council"; or, in other words, an evolution from the time when kings ruled through the agency of ministers to that time when ministers began to govern through the instrumentality of the Crown. This change took centuries to come about. The conflict reached a climax after the Stuarts came to the throne in 1603. They claimed the right to rule as divine-right monarchs, but this claim was challenged in a revolution in 1642. While the first attempt to limit royal power produced the Commonwealth, parliamentary institutions were not easily established. The Stuarts were restored, only to be again overthrown. The final solution took power from one, the king, and distributed it among many, the ministers.

This distribution was codified with the passage of the Bill of Rights in 1689 and the Act of Settlement in 1701. Beginning with the reign of William and Mary (1689–1694), whom Parliament *invited* to reign, the pace of the restriction of royal power was increased. It was Anne (1702–1714) who learned that sovereigns must rule with the favor of one or the other of the two great political parties, and she was the last British ruler to veto an act of Parliament. She was also the last monarch to attend a meeting of the cabinet because by the end of her reign the cabinet had ceased being the personal adjunct of the monarch and had become the spokesman of the dominant political power in Parliament. The pressure of parliamentary majorities upon the Crown's choice of ministers had become irresistible by the time the Hanoverians arrived, and the situation was aided immeasurably by the inability of George I to speak English. This inability forced him to rely upon his ministers in order to rule, and this reliance set a precedent henceforth impossible to ignore or undo.

By the beginning of the reign of George I, royal prerogative had already been brought into legal bounds. The only authority which remained to be checked involved the king's discretionary power, and above all, the right to appoint and retain his own personal ministers. Considering the distribution of power between Parliament and king as it evolved during the 1800's, at the end of the reign of George IV in 1830, the monarch no longer had this discretionary power. Thus by the time Victoria came to the throne in 1837, the constitutional monarchical system had evolved to what it is today, and the extent of the political power of the Crown was no longer an issue. True enough, Victoria in her later years meddled a great deal, and her ministers listened to her with the courtesy that age, experience, a measure of wisdom, and affection are able to command. But she never carried the day on any major political issue, and she reigned in strict compliance with Bagehot's observation that constitutional monarchs may warn, advise, and encourage but do nothing more:

> Broadly speaking since the death of Queen Victoria royal intervention has been used only to advocate the unity of the nation, at times when party and group warfare have threatened to cause violent dissention, and to promote "national" and imperial interests in international affairs. All depends upon personality and talent but the hereditary, symbolic and . . . social status of the Crown enable it to exercise a unifying influence in cabinet counsel. It is not a power behind the cabinet but *by* and *with* the cabinet, and, of course, never against its determined will.[2]

[2] Herman Finer, *The Theory and Practice of Modern Government* (New York: Henry Holt & Co., The Dial Press, 1949).

In Belgium, the monarchy underwent a belated evolution (one coming *after* the establishment of the constitutional monarchical system) that was complicated by the duality of its function. As the lower classes became socially and politically articulate, their demands became increasingly more stubborn, and their intransigence threatened to disrupt the political process; this was particularly true between 1920 and 1940. At the same time, these classes demanded a larger share in this process. As they entered Parliament it was logical that this share would take the form of increased parliamentary authority. In the reapportionment of a predetermined whole, in this case the entirety of governmental power set forth in the Constitution, an expansion in one share results in an automatic contraction in another. An increase in the power of the popularly elected Parliament would therefore indicate a decrease in that of the monarchical executive. After World War I, the Socialists took the initiative in pressing for this redistribution, not through constitutional amendment but by political attrition that utilized the party and the workings of the cabinet system. Belgian Socialists have always supported the monarchy (the reality of Belgian political existence demands this); yet theoretically Socialists are republicans. Therefore, the closer the monarchical system approaches the republican in function, the easier it is for the Socialists to reconcile theory with practice. But the Socialists failed to understand the dual nature of the Belgian monarchy: that is to say, one could not weaken the executive powers of the monarch without reducing his capacity to serve as the source of national unity.

Elements of Division in Belgium

Although Belgium came into existence as an independent nation in 1831, the Belgian provinces which formed the nation had belonged to the dukes of Burgundy from the reign of

Philip the Bold to that of Charles the Bold, i.e., from 1384 until 1477. After the abdication of Charles V as Holy Roman Emperor, the area was ruled first by Spain, next by Austria, then by France, and finally, between 1815 and 1830, by Holland. Throughout these centuries the two major ethnic groups, i.e., the Flemings and the Walloons, maintained their identity, and at the time of the revolution against Holland in 1830 these groups were still separate. The Walloons trace their ancestry to the original Belgic tribes of Celtic origin, and the Flemings to the Franks, who later settled the same general area but who were prevented by the forests of Brabant and Flanders, and by the Roman soldiers, from penetrating into what would be today Walloon territory. This separation has been maintained in part even to the present.

The revolution against Holland in 1830 and the establishment of the Belgian state in 1831 had been brought about by the combined efforts of Catholics and Liberals, who buried their differences long enough to create a nation and see it through the difficult years of infancy.[3] From 1815 to 1830 the Catholics had suffered what they considered the intolerable educational policies of the Dutch king, Willem I, who wished to establish state control over all religious activity including education. The Liberals, on the other hand, had suffered what they considered intolerable regulations regarding civil liberties, particularly freedom of the press. The unwillingness of the Dutch to make concessions provoked the Catholics and Liberals to create the Union for the peaceful redressing of their grievances.[4] Holland's continued failure to respond changed the Union into a revolutionary organization. This Catholic-Liberal alliance was successful for approximately fif-

[3] For a detailed account of this period and of Belgian history in general, see Frans van Kalken, *Histoire de Belgique des origines à 1914* (Bruxelles: Office de Publicité, 1944); and Henri Pirenne, *Histoire de Belgique* (6 vols.; Bruxelles: H. Lamertin, 1909–1926).

[4] Unionism was the name given to the co-operation of Liberals and Catholics from the years immediately preceding the revolution until 1846.

teen years after the revolution in 1830 but began to break apart over the problem of state support for Catholic schools; it finally collapsed in 1846. From that date until 1884 governments alternated between Catholic and Liberal until the Catholics came to power in 1884 and governed without interruption until World War I.

This split between Liberals and Catholics, though a significant division in Belgian society, was a break along one dimension only. The ruling class, whether Catholic or Liberal, remained socially and economically unified and shared a common outlook.

During the 1880's a new group came into being—the Socialists. Because of voting qualifications the great majority of the lower classes was disfranchised, thus confining Socialists to non-political activity. But their demands began to increase in volume and their voice was heard through the trade unions and workingmen's associations, co-operatives, and mutual societies. Even before the rise of the Socialists the Catholic lower classes had begun to voice their discontent. Conferences were held at Malines in 1884 and 1887 and in Liége in 1886 that resulted in reluctant approval by the Catholic oligarchy of social and economic, but not political, concessions to the masses. These concessions were minimal, however, because the philosophic dispute between conservative and progressive Catholics remained unresolved until 1891.

After the promulgation in 1891 of *Rerum Novarum,* the charter of Catholic workers which sanctioned progressive social and economic theory, the Catholics in power began to move slowly toward the social and political democratization of Belgium. The electoral law of April 18, 1893, the first since the adoption of the Constitution in 1831, established male suffrage. Each man over twenty-five years of age was given the vote, but a married man paying a minimum property tax, a widower with a child, a businessman, a man living on his invested capital, or a man with a university diploma, received one or two additional ballots. As an outgrowth of the liberalization of the franchise the last decade of the nineteenth century saw the beginnings of social legislation, but change continued at a gradual pace. The new electoral law continued to discriminate in favor of the man of means and stable position so that the Socialists and the lower-class Catholics remained politically weak. On the eve of World War I the political balance of power was more or less as it had been since the 1880's. Nevertheless, new social divisions became apparent. The socioeconomic split between upper and lower classes (always existent but now beginning to widen) had been added to the religious division among the upper classes, a division which had been compounded by the philosophic differences among Catholics themselves. And among the lower classes, too, religious differences increased as Catholic workingmen abandoned their church for socialism.

After World War I universal manhood suffrage was established, which gave the vote to all the lower classes.[5] As a result of the first elections held under the broadened franchise, the Liberal party was replaced by the Socialist as the second major party, and the Catholic party was forced to reorganize in order to allow the lower classes a share in the party's organization and management. The prewar economic and social divisions were now solidified politically.

Parallels for these social and political cleavages may be found throughout western Europe. In particular the divisions resembled those of France, where the religious, socioeconomic, and political issues formed a grid of interacting forces.[6] They were in contrast, however, to those of England, where major

[5] This change in the franchise did not come about through legislative initiative but as the result of a promise made by King Albert (with ministerial approval) in his address from the throne on November 22, 1919, in which he commented that it would be unjust to allow the profiteers of the war to continue to enjoy the privilege of plural voting while those who had fought in the trenches could cast only a single ballot.

[6] For a thorough discussion of these divisions in France see David Thompson, *Democracy in France* (New York, 1949); and in particular Philip Williams, *Politics in Postwar France* (London: Longmans Green and Co., 1954).

changes had come about one by one and had allowed time for national adjustment between the alterations in society. The Reformation settled the religious issue comfortably before the question of regime demanded an answer, and this in turn was settled before the economic fractures resulting from the industrial revolution had to be mended. In France, on the other hand, the first two issues, i.e., the religious and that of regime, erupted with the revolution in 1789 and were still unsettled when the country split economically because of industrialization. For this reason, the economic Left and Right in France were not necessarily congruent with the classic Left and Right of the religious vocabulary, and until recently the question of regime could still make and break politicians.

The situation in Belgium was analogous to that in France, but not as complex. The question of regime has not divided the Belgians in the same manner as it has the French. The Belgian constitutional monarchy grew out of a revolution which found the Catholic Right and the Liberal Left fighting on the same side. As in France, the religious issue was embodied in the combustible *question scolaire,* but the socio-economic issues in Belgium did not result in the same political fragmentation so characteristic of France. The Liberals, conservative economically but politically Left, i.e., anticlerical, had their counterpart in the French Radicals, but the Catholic Right in Belgium differed from the Catholic Right in France. In France, the Catholic Right was conservative politically as well as economically and therefore afforded no voice for the radical Catholic working classes. In Belgium, both elements were accommodated, admittedly with strain and imperfectly, in the Catholic party. After the promulgation of *Rerum Novarum* in 1891 the Catholic Right began to make concessions to the left wing of the party because the conservative Catholics feared concessions less than the creation of a labor party which would unite Socialists and radical Catholics. Perhaps the most conspicuous difference between France and

Belgium was the language split, a geographical, cultural, and linguistic fissure which cut across all the other divisions in Belgian society.

During the 1920's the Flemish-Walloon antipathy was rekindled. Throughout the nineteenth century the Flemings had remained second-class citizens within their own country. The free use of both Flemish and French had been guaranteed by the Constitution, but a reaction against former Dutch rule and especially against the linguistic policies of Willem I resulted in French becoming the official language.[7] The civil service, the army, the bar, education, the courts, the higher clergy, the aristocracy, all became French-oriented. Even the Flemish nobility and upper bourgeoisie spoke French exclusively, so that within Flanders itself those who would have formed the nucleus of a provincial culture abandoned their linguistic heritage. Throughout Belgium a change in social status was geared to a knowledge of French and the cultivation of a French *esprit;* to be identified with things Flemish was a mark of cultural inferiority. But among Flemish intellectuals and among the minor Flemish clergy a reaction set in against this subordinacy during the last quarter of the nineteenth century. On August 16, 1873, a law was passed which required criminal trials in Flanders to be conducted in Flemish.[8] In 1898 the De Vriendt-Coremans law granted to Flemish equal status with French. This law required official governmental publications to be written in both languages and required both languages to appear on stamps, currency, public buildings, and early in the 1900's other laws were passed which regulated the use of both languages in Parliament, in the civil service, in the courts, and in secondary education.

[7] Flemish is the same language as Dutch but is pronounced differently. The well-educated Fleming speaks pure Dutch, however.

[8] In the army, where French was the official language, a Flemish peasant drafted into the service was later court-martialed and sentenced to death without ever fully understanding the nature of his crime. His accusers, his defenders, and his judge spoke only French.

Beginning with the 1920's the Flemings, taking inspiration from the same reasoning which had condemned the undemocratic electoral laws, demanded full equality in all other aspects of national life. The law of July 31, 1921, compelled cabinet ministers to exchange communications with provincial authorities in the language of the region. In 1932 laws were passed which required the use of both languages in all ministries. An educational law stipulated that in primary schools the parent no longer had the right to choose the language of instruction, thereby delivering a serious blow to the snob appeal of French. *Moedertaal-Voertaal* ("mother tongue-instruction tongue") was replaced by *Landstaal-Voertaal* ("regional tongue-instruction tongue"). Another law required all defendants to be tried and judged in their mother tongue; the army was made bilingual, and a Flemish section in the Royal Military Academy was created for the training of Flemish officers. But the most important step toward cultural equality was the establishment of an all-Flemish university by converting to Flemish the French-speaking state university at Ghent.[9] Education could now be obtained exclusively in Flemish from primary through professional school. At long last the Flemings felt they were free of the seduction of French culture, at least officially.

It has been necessary to dwell at length on this cultural-social-linguistic scission because it gives depth to the split between Flanders and Wallonia over the Leopold affair. The Flemings were still on the defensive at the time of the royal question. As often happens with "minority" groups, the reaction against the former "oppressors" came not during the years of discrimination but during the first years of newly won equality. After 1945 Leopold III became identified as the Flemish king by the Walloons who, by the time of the royal question, had begun to fear the encroachment of the Flemish

[9] Following this, many courses at the private universities of Louvain and Brussels were offered in Flemish. At Louvain today all classes in all faculties are offered in both languages.

language and culture. Since it is the Flemings who voluntarily learn French and not, in general, the Walloons who learn Flemish, the laws which require all governmental personnel to be bilingual were working to the advantage of the Flemings. The French-speaking Belgians feared a *flamandisation* of Belgian life.

The sensitivity of the French-speaking Belgians regarding their inherited culture can be fully understood only by living among the Belgians. There exists a contempt among the Walloons for their Flemish brothers that can best be demonstrated by recalling French contempt for non-French culture and then multiplying this contempt severalfold. The French at least are secure in their culture; the Walloons never relax their vigilance. It is important to know this about the Leopold affair: if the Catholic Flemings had succeeded in returning Leopold III to his throne, it would have been the first time in Belgian history that Flanders had imposed its will upon Wallonia and Brussels. Given the recent cultural, social, and linguistic renaissance of Flanders, this political phenomenon might have been more than Wallonia could have tolerated.

Leopold III and His Relationship to the Monarchy

The power of the king is set forth in the Constitution in Articles 26, 27, and 29, and the enumeration of these powers appears in Articles 60–78. Of these, those most pertinent to this study are the following:

ARTICLE 26—The Legislative power is exercised collectively by the King, the House of Representatives, and the Senate.[10]

[10] In the houses of Parliament there are representatives from Flanders and Wallonia. The capital is considered a unit apart, *l'agglomération bruxelloise,* and elects either French-speaking or Flemish-speaking dele-

ARTICLE 27—Initiative belongs to each of the three branches of legislative power.

ARTICLE 29—To the King belongs the executive power as it is regulated by the Constitution.

ARTICLE 63—The person of the King is inviolable; his ministers are responsible.

ARTICLE 64—No act of the King can have effect unless it is countersigned by a minister, which minister, by his signing, becomes responsible.

ARTICLE 65—The King appoints and dismisses his ministers.

ARTICLE 68—The King commands the forces on land and sea, declares war, makes treaties of peace, alliance, and commerce. He informs the Chambers as soon as the interest and safety of the State permit, presenting to them pertinent communications. . . .

ARTICLE 69—The King sanctions and promulgates the laws.

ARTICLE 71—The King has the right to dissolve the Chambers, either simultaneously or separately. . . .

ARTICLE 72—The King can adjourn the Chambers. . . .

ARTICLE 80—The King comes of age at eighteen years inclusive. He takes possession of the throne only after having solemnly sworn before the Chambers sitting in joint session the following oath:

"I swear to observe the Constitution and the laws of the Belgian people, to maintain national independence, and the integrity of the territory."

ARTICLE 82—If the King finds it impossible to reign, his ministers, after having established this impossibility, immediately convoke the chambers. . . .

---

gates. This is so not because of a federal system, which does not exist, but simply because no exclusively French-speaking candidate could get elected in Flanders, nor an exclusively Flemish-speaking candidate in Wallonia.

ARTICLE 83—The Regency can be conferred only upon one person.

The Constitution grants the monarch extensive power. In theory he is able to refuse to approve legislation, to appoint and dismiss his personal ministers, to adjourn Parliament, or to dissolve it either in whole or in part.[11] He commands the armed forces and is responsible for the maintenance of the nation's independence and its territorial integrity. His power would be almost total if it were not for Articles 63 and 64. Yet, even considering these Articles, the king occupies a position of great authority, far in excess of the nineteenth-century British model. The British monarch, according to Bagehot, has only three rights: the right to be consulted, the right to encourage, and the right to warn. The first two Belgian monarchs, Leopold I and Leopold II, did not hesitate to use their constitutional powers even though a gradual evolution was already taking place in the conception of authority under Articles 65, 71, and 72.[12] The evolution was delayed, however, for several reasons. The first was the personality of Leopold II, who reigned from 1864 until 1909 and saw himself as a king in the grand manner. Even Belgians say, and many still despise him in the 1960's, that he was born out of his time; they liken him in spirit to Louis XIV.[13] Second, the conservative Catholics who governed uninterruptedly from 1884 until 1914 were not philosophically opposed to a strong monarch. Third, the

---

[11] The cabinet is responsible to both houses of Parliament.

[12] The best biographies of the first two Leopolds have been written by Count Louis de Lichtervelde: *Léopold Ier* (Bruxelles: Librairie Albert Dewit, 1929); *Léopold II* (Bruxelles: Editions Universitaires, 1926).

[13] Many Belgians have never forgiven Leopold II for having forced the Congo on them. Whether rightly or wrongly, they have always considered it to be a drain rather than a source of profit. But what the Belgians have really never forgiven Leopold II in regard to the Congo is the fact that he was in Paris visiting his mistress on the day the transfer took place, dramatizing once again the aphorism he coined to describe his people and his land: *petit gens, petit pays.*

Socialists who rejected a strong monarchy did not become a political power until after 1920.

It was during the reign of King Albert, 1909–1934, that the position of the monarch was noticeably altered. Albert discontinued several practices by which Belgian sovereigns had historically identified themselves publicly with policy. The New Year's reception and address at the palace, the political banquets, and the personal speeches delivered on important public occasions were abandoned so that the people lost "political" contact with their sovereign. He became the beloved symbol of national unity, visible yet aloof, a living legend which had started to grow during World War I and which Albert chose never to mar. The people became accustomed to an apparently passive king. He was the first Belgian monarch to rule in the manner described and accepted as constitutional by modern theorists.[14] Events during the second half of his reign were of a nature peaceful enough not to demand his active and overt participation. Albert died in 1934 only months before Belgium entered into a period of crisis that did not end until 1950, the year of Leopold's abdication.

It is impossible to say whether Albert would have met the crises which began in 1935 any differently from the way his son did. We do not know if Albert reigned as he did because of disposition alone or because events were auspicious. We do know that when his successor was forced by circumstances to act as the Constitution allowed, he was denounced as an autocrat and repudiated by his people. We cannot deny that Leopold III acted as he did largely because of his personality. To him the power of the monarch should be as it appeared in the Constitution: strong and positive. Leopold was unrealistic in his condemnation of the course of political evolution and the workings of party government; yet we cannot ignore the contribution of events which nourished his bias.

---

[14] For an excellent discussion of this manner see Walter Bagehot, *The English Constitution* (New York: D. Appleton & Co., 1884), Chapter IV.

In 1935 the failure of the Catholic-Liberal government under Georges Theunis to cope with the economic crisis compelled Leopold to call Paul Van Zeeland from outside Parliament to become prime minister.[15] The extent of Van Zeeland's success and the gratitude which Belgians felt toward him were demonstrated in April, 1937, when he became the candidate supported by the Catholic, Liberal, Socialist, and Communist parties in a special election in Brussels. In May, 1936, the Rexist party, a fascist organization under the leadership of Léon Degrelle, won twenty-one parliamentary seats in its first national election. By early 1937, however, the attitude of the Belgians toward the Rexist party had begun to sour, owing primarily to an anti-Rexist campaign organized and sustained by the Government. In April, 1937, as a test of strength, Degrelle himself chose to run for a Brussels parliamentary seat. The four major parties asked Van Zeeland to campaign against him. The Prime Minister's triumph surpassed expectation, yet in October of the same year he was compelled to resign because of a scandal in the *Banque Nationale,* a scandal in which it is conceded that he had played an innocent part. His enemies, primarily the Rexists and their parliamentary ally, the National Flemish party, used this incident to force him out of politics. This repudiation of a public servant who had come to the nation's rescue only two years before gave a sharp blow to Leopold's already waning faith in parliamentary procedure. The events which took place during the following two years further darkened his view and led him increasingly to equate governmental stability with the strength of his own position.

From October 28 until November 30, 1937, Leopold labored to find a prime minister acceptable to Parliament, where the use of "exclusives"[16] was leading to total governmental paraly-

[15] See Carl-Henrik Höjer, *Le régime parlementaire belge de 1918 à 1940* (Stockholm: Almqvist & Wiksells Bokryckeri AB, 1946). This is the single best account of parliamentary history for the prewar period.
[16] An "exclusive" was the means whereby a party refused to consider

sis. First, Leopold called two Socialists successively to form a cabinet. The Socialists were the largest party at this time, although they lacked a majority. Emile Vandervelde, the "grand old man" of Belgian Socialism refused to try; Henri De Man, the president of the Socialist party, failed because the Liberals feared his economic policies, which actually differed very little from Van Zeeland's. Leopold then asked two Catholics successively, Cyrille Van Overbergh, who begged off because of health, and Hubert Pierlot, who was unable to overcome the opposition of the Socialists. Next, Paul-Henri Spaak, a Socialist, was summoned by the King, but the Catholics turned him down because the Socialists had turned down Pierlot. Leopold was forced to call a meeting of the leaders of the three major parties. After long consultation, a Liberal candidate was agreed upon, Paul-Emil Janson. This compromise lasted until May 12, 1938, when the Prime Minister was forced to resign because he found himself without a cabinet. One-by-one four of his Catholic ministers left the Cabinet because of a split in Catholic ranks over the remedies to be taken to solve the economic problems that had begun in September and October, 1937.[17] In addition, one other Catholic left because of illness and another died. The failure of the coalition occurred without the Cabinet being either repudiated by Parliament or dismissed by the King.

Leopold then turned to Spaak to form a government. The latter's skill and Parliament's reluctance to repeat the cat-and-mouse politics which had left Belgium without a government for thirty days four months previously enabled him to create a viable government, but it lasted only until February, 1939.

---

a particular man for a particular ministry. It was primarily a retaliatory measure. As each of the three major parties increased its list of "exclusives," the function of government came to a halt. No one would agree with anyone else.

[17] During this period of parliamentary confusion, Hitler had moved into Austria (March 13, 1938), and France had devalued the franc, once again threatening Belgium's economic stability.

The new crisis had begun in January when the Government appointed Dr. Martens, a Fleming, to the Flemish Academy of Medicine. Martens, who had been a collaborator during World War I, had been condemned to death, but was pardoned in 1920. In Belgium there is no issue more delicate than *incivisme*, the term applied to the activity of pro-German Belgians during the two world wars. The Walloons claim that the Flemings have a monopoly on treason, while the Flemings counter with the proverb of the mote and the beam and protest that collaboration laws discriminate against them. The Flemings, therefore, interpreted the Martens appointment as a partial vindication of their claims. The Walloons, on the other hand, used it to renew their anti-Flemish charges. Spaak sought to defend his appointment by stating that he never would have appointed the doctor if he had any reason to doubt his loyalty. This defense notwithstanding, Spaak paid for his indiscretion by being forced to resign.

Once again Leopold was compelled to enter the political arena in order to find a prime minister. On February 23, Hubert Pierlot, a Catholic, formed a government that collapsed four days later because of the Martens affair. On March 6 Leopold dissolved Parliament. Elections were held on April 2. Elsewhere in Europe, between late February and early April, 1939, while Belgium indulged in internal petty bickering, Slovakia had proclaimed her independence from Czechoslovakia, and on March 14, the German armies had moved into Prague and installed themselves in Bohemia-Moravia. On March 22, Germany acquired Memel.

On February 2, at a meeting of the Council of Ministers, King Leopold took the Government to task for the condition of Belgian political life:

> Postwar circumstances and events have modified our political parties by weakening their unity. Their fragmentation has had serious consequences; the very principles

of parliamentary government have been threatened. The majority system has been upset by the forced collaboration of several parties to form a government and by the suppression of a normal and necessary opposition.

Having become a miniature of Parliament, where all political nuances of the majority must be represented and proportioned, the ministeries are becoming more and more ephemeral and difficult to form.

The growing influence of political parties is being substituted for constitutional power. Ministers become the agents of their party; governments break up and resign without being turned out by Parliament.[18]

Leopold commented further, pointing out that ministers once appointed are "agents of the executive power" and not party representatives. He then raised his voice against the growing practice of the government of submitting decrees, appointments, and enabling legislation for his signature after they had already been made public or leaked to the press. He stated:

> Article 64 of the Constitution stipulates that no act of the king can take effect until countersigned by a minister. That stipulation guarantees that no one shall ever uncover the king. More and more, certain practices are being undertaken which are diametrically opposed to that principle. . . . Those practices no longer permit the Chief of State to fulfill his constitutional role; he is no longer covered by his ministers; it is he, on the contrary, who covers them.

[18] *Contribution à l'étude de la question royale* (Bruxelles: Groupement national belge en collaboration avec la Centrale belge de Documentation, n.d.), p. 79. This will be cited henceforth as the *Contribution*.

The *Contribution* is a collection of *publicly available* documents and publications grouped chronologically to aid comprehension. The *Groupement national belge* was a non-partisan organization sympathetic to Leopold III. It seems to have collapsed after the royal affair came to an end.

I can no longer permit the Government to demand my urgent signature for important decrees without allowing me the time to study them, to reflect upon them, and to formulate an opinion concerning them. Those who drew up the Constitution certainly did not wish that the role of the Head of State should be reduced to that of the servile legislator of decisions taken without him by members of his government.[19]

On the day Leopold signed the order of dissolution, March 6, 1939, he wrote a letter to Prime Minister Hubert Pierlot in which he reiterated his criticism of party politics but denied the allegation that he wanted to impose his own will on the Government:

If the principles of our national charter are thus forgotten, the Head of State is no longer able to play the role which falls to him, and, highly improperly, the Crown is implicated when it should be solely the ministers who are responsible before the houses of Parliament for the acts carrying the signature of the king. As for wishing to superimpose upon the political and legal responsibility of the ministers a kind of moral responsibility of the king himself, that is a false conception which will only confuse public opinion. Those who on certain occasions echo malicious or simply tendentious statements risk, without perhaps suspecting it, committing an injustice regarding the only citizen in the kingdom to whom are forbidden the means given every man to defend his opinions and his acts.[20]

The elections resulted in a return to partial stability resting upon the three major parties. The Rexists now numbered only four; the Communists, nine; and the National Flemish, fifteen.

[19] *Ibid.*, p. 80. The word *couvrir* ("to cover") is the term used to indicate the action of a government when it assumes responsibility for the actions of the monarch who, constitutionally speaking, could only act on the advice of responsible ministers.

[20] *Ibid.*, p. 85.

Yet the three major parties still found it impossible to agree on a prime minister. Once again Leopold was forced to speak:

> Constitutional monarchy is based upon the principle of a rigorous separation of power. It supposes alongside a Parliament which legislates and controls, an executive which governs. The executive power belongs to the king (Article 29 of the Constitution) who appoints and dismisses his ministers (Article 65) who alone are responsible before Parliament.
>
> Now as the executive power has been weakened the role of the state has not ceased growing. Thus, by a paradoxical contradiction, the more the state is obliged to act, the less it is capable of doing so. . . .
>
> The first necessary condition, that upon which depends, I do not hesitate to affirm, the very fate of our regime, is the restoration, in all its independence and in all its capacity of action, of a truly responsible executive power— that is to say, formed by men who are able to assure the governing of the country throughout an entire legislative period, without finding themselves hindered in their action by the orders from parties, by decisions of political groups and subgroups, or by electoral preoccupation.
>
> Of all the reforms that must be realized, the most important is that of the mentality of the men in power, the ministers. Without this reform, which demands no new legislation, the rest are vain and impossible.[21]

On April 17, 1939, the Catholics and Liberals formed a coalition government, and the Socialists went into opposition. On September 5, following the outbreak of war in Poland, Leopold took steps that led to the formation of a tripartite cabinet which governed, but not without mishap, until war came to Belgium in May, 1940. On April 25, 1940, sixteen days before the German invasion, the Government offered its

[21] *Ibid.,* p. 86.

resignation to the King. The cause of the crisis was the refusal of a handful of Liberal members of Parliament to approve the public-school budget because of the operation of certain linguistic laws. Without even losing parliamentary support, Pierlot offered the Cabinet's resignation to Leopold, who refused it:

> At the moment when the army stands vigilant guard at our frontiers and when the international situation makes it imperative for all Belgians to draw more closely together in union, it is certainly not the time for a ministerial crisis involving questions of internal politics.
>
> I would go counter to the superior interest of the country in accepting the resignation of the Government following a recent vote in the Senate confirming that our foreign policy meets with the approval of almost the entire nation.[22]

"I would go counter to the superior interests of the country" —these were indeed prophetic words. Exactly one month from the date he wrote to Pierlot, Leopold cut relations with the Government and within another three days surrendered his army and himself to the Germans, guided in his actions by the same philosophy which prompted him to refuse the resignation and which had shaped his actions since 1935: his personal notion of the greater good of Belgium.

Leopold's Philosophy of Kingship

It is necessary to analyze what Leopold conceived to be the true function of the monarchy, for it is in that inquiry where one must search for the rationale that motivated and governed his personal interference in Belgium's domestic and international affairs. Leopold never publicly developed this reasoning,

[22] *Ibid.*, p. 115.

but Louis Wodon, the King's *chef de cabinet* from 1934 until 1940, on various occasions expressed his opinion regarding what he considered to be the real function of the monarchy. It should not strain credulity to assume that men who have been intimately associated for many years should share common opinions, particularly when one of the men is a king and the other his servant.[23] It is legitimate to assume that the peculiar theories of Wodon reflected the thoughts of Leopold himself concerning the monarch and his relation to the state.

Wodon distinguished between the function of the monarch as an executive and his function as Head of State.[24] He based this distinction on the oath taken by Belgian kings upon accession to the throne: "I swear to observe the Constitution and the laws of the Belgian people, to maintain national independence and the integrity of the territory." Wodon reasoned that the oath implied a royal position over and above the Constitution, a position which could be understood by reading the document as a whole.

That which in reality establishes and consecrates the royal pre-eminence is the title of Head of State which belongs to the king and in which are concentrated and synthesized the allocation of duties which fall to him over and beyond the legislative and executive. These result from a combination of constitutional texts intelligently understood, of the spirit of the whole which flows from it, and finally of the traditional unwritten rules which form a very notable part of our public law. . . . Every constitution supposes essential elements which are anterior and supe-

[23] The word "servant" is eminently valid, for the *chef de cabinet* is the personal choice of the king, not subject to ministerial approval.

[24] This distinction, a standard one made by authors on constitutional monarchy (see Herman Finer, *The Theory and Practice of Modern Government*) has a meaning unique to Wodon. He does not see the monarch as the Head of State impersonating the state on gala occasions as do other authors, including Finer. Wodon sees the Head of State as a position embodying the state and speaking for it on a higher plane than the constitutional or parliamentary.

rior to it. Such is the case of the existence of the state and
its independence. The latter implies the former. These
would be sustained in vain by a strict and literal interpretation of certain texts scrupulously interpreted; it is reasonable that it would lead to conclusions and results which
would go counter to that independence and that existence.

If the oath alludes to objectives other than the Constitution and the laws, it is exactly because these objectives are
not revealed by the texts of the charter which presupposes
them and which go beyond that document. From this it
follows that it is only by condemnable sophistry that one
would be able to understand these texts in a sense destruc-
tive to the elements at the base of the Constitution itself. It
should be noted that the oath is a personal act of the king,
and there is no question of ministerial countersigning.[25]

Wodon makes this further comment comparing the king to a
father, to the head of a family:

> Regarding the moral mission of the king it is permissible
> to point to a certain analogy between his role and that of
> a father, or more generally, of parents in a family. The
> family is, of course, a legal institution as is the state. But
> what would a family be where everything was limited
> among those who compose it to simply legal relationships?
> In a family when one considers only legal relationships one
> comes very close to a breakdown in the moral ties founded
> on reciprocal affection without which a family would be
> like any other fragile association.[26]

It is not difficult to grasp Leopold's opinions regarding the
monarchy. He understood its purpose; he understood its in-

[25] Louis Wodon, "Sur le rôle du roi comme chef de l'état dans les cas
de défaillances constitutionnelles," *Bulletin de l'Académie Royale de
Belgique*, 1941, pp. 211–14.
[26] Louis Wodon, "Du recours pour excès de pouvoir devant la Constitution belge," *Bulletin de l'Académie Royal de Belgique*, 3ᵉ Série, XXIV
(décembre 5, 1938), 542.

dispensability to national unity. It is difficult, however, to accept his outdated philosophy, one which, for all its good intention, contained the seeds of disastrous consequences. One cannot read Wodon without the shock of realization that he wrote not for the seventeenth but for the twentieth century. Leopold seemed to have dismissed an unavoidable reality—the gradual evolution that had taken place in the concept of monarchical power. This evolution had been arrested in Belgium because of the several factors which were discussed above. By the 1930's, however, the causes of the delay had been removed and the evolution could continue, this time more rapidly. Yet, the very factors that allowed the evolution to move forward released completely the divisive elements which only a strong monarchy could keep in check. King Leopold's behavior before, during, and after the war can be understood only by keeping this paradox in mind.

CHAPTER 2

THE POLICY OF INDEPENDENCE-NEUTRALITY

THE POLICY OF "independence-neutrality" has been identified by the opponents of King Leopold as a personal design imposed by him on an unwilling Government. During the royal affair this opinion was given wide publicity and was used to strengthen the case against the King. Nevertheless, this course of action was the natural consequence of the interplay of two phenomena: the first, the failure of collective security and of international agreements (i.e., the failure of the League of Nations and of the Locarno Pact) to assure Belgium's safety; the second, the internal divisions peculiar to Belgium. The plan, though introduced by Leopold and identified with him, was accepted by the Government and remained the policy of each succeeding government until war came to Belgium in May, 1940.

The Collapse of Collective Security and International Alliance

The workings of European politics that had forced a policy of neutrality upon Belgium from 1830 until 1914 compelled her after World War I to find guarantees for her safety in collective security and international alliance. The bases of this security were the League of Nations and the Locarno Pact.[1] The obligations assumed by Belgium under the League and Locarno were out of proportion to her size and strength, but they were supportable so long as the conditions established by the Versailles Treaty remained stable. They would have dangerous consequences in the event that the status quo were altered.

By the mid-1930's one of the bases for Belgian security had collapsed. The collective protection afforded by the League of Nations had been a dead letter since the Sino-Japanese dispute in 1931, and events in Europe and Africa since that time marked the final disintegration of the organization's power and authority. In January, 1933, Hitler became Chancellor and in the following October took Germany out of the League and out of the Disarmament Conference. On March 16, 1935, Germany repudiated the military, naval, and air clauses of the Treaty of Versailles and announced that conscription would be reintroduced. At the same time Hitler began to build a military air force. Belgium watched uneasily across an all too narrow Rhineland as the armed strength of Germany increased; yet, though the League could no longer be relied upon to maintain European order, the Locarno Pact made this zone inviolable and Belgium felt relatively secure.

On March 7, 1936, Germany reoccupied the Rhineland.[2] The Locarno powers failed to act. Shortly afterward Prime Minister Van Zeeland went to London to meet with the repre-

---

[1] In 1920 Belgium had signed a treaty with France which fixed the details of military co-operation in the event of fresh aggression on the part of Germany. The treaty for all practical purposes had been absorbed into the more encompassing Locarno Pact; until March 6, 1936, however, the day before the German reoccupation of the Rhineland, the Franco-Belgian treaty was a binding obligation upon the nations and so might be considered a third base of security.

[2] The Franco-Belgain pact was dissolved by France on March 6, 1936.

sentatives of France, Italy, and Great Britain and ask them what they intended to do in order to keep their word and to protect Belgium while protecting themselves, and with themselves the whole civilized world.[3] Eden made it clear that British opinion would never sanction military action whose purpose it was to expel Germans from the Rhineland, their historic soil. On this question Flandin represented a divided French government and a nation ill-prepared to go to war. Italy would not call Germany to task only six months following the beginning of her own Ethiopian campaign. As a result, Van Zeeland was forced to return to Belgium and inform his nation that the great powers would do nothing for the moment, but that negotiations would be entered into whose results would be binding upon Belgium. He had agreed at London to follow the initiative of Great Britain and France in opening negotiations with Germany for the creation of a new Rhine pact and had promised Belgian military aid in the event of further German hostility.

In the meantime Belgium lay exposed and committed beyond her strength—committed by the military agreements made at London and by Locarno, which still bound her to France, Great Britain, and Italy, but exposed because her geographic position was no longer protected by German participation in Locarno. All that remained was the word of Britain and France to renegotiate with Germany and the pledge of Britain alone made on April 1 that she would guarantee Belgian territorial integrity, sources of little comfort to Belgium in the light of what had recently happened along the Rhine.

Belgium had not allowed this situation to find her totally unprepared militarily. Already in the early 1930's the Belgian government had seen the direction in which European politics

[3] Emile Cammaerts, *The Prisoner at Laeken, Fact and Legend* (London: The Cresset Press, 1941), p. 96.

was moving. From 1932, Albert Devèze, the Liberal minister of defense in the de Broqueville Cabinet,[4] had taken steps to improve the nation's military position. He had mechanized the artillery and the cavalry, introduced modern weapons, and in 1934, created frontier guard units, including the *Chasseurs Ardennais,* an elite career group that rode bicycles and had, also, some motorcycles. But his policy of conscription met insurmountable opposition. He had wanted to lengthen the period of service in order that the army might receive better training, but the Catholic party was opposed and unwilling to make concessions. Its opposition was not based upon moral ground; it was a purely political issue. The strength of the Catholic party lay in Flanders. The Flemings have been historically opposed to all things French [5] and had resented the treaties which bound Belgium to France, particularly the Franco-Belgian treaty of 1920, following whose stipulations Belgian and French troops had marched together into the Ruhr in 1923. Flanders was less opposed to Locarno because this treaty parceled out responsibility more broadly, but the Flemish population had never been happy with any of the agreements to which France was a partner. Thus the proposal to change the conscription laws met Flemish resistance so long as there remained the possibility that Belgian soldiers might fight for the benefit of France. Flanders could do nothing to alter the *fait accompli* of Locarno, but it was determined to obstruct any policy which would have as its possible result further military co-operation with France.

In November, 1935, the general staff of the Belgian army, alarmed by German rearmament and convinced that Britain and France did not take these developments seriously, laid before King Leopold a program for national defense, a program which received his complete approval as commander-in-

---

[4] The de Broqueville Cabinet was a Catholic-Liberal coalition.
[5] This was in large part a reaction against that condition of inferiority spoken of in Chapter 1.

chief of the armed forces. The project was next presented to Parliament, but, once again, because of the provisions for conscription, the Catholic party refused to approve it. To impress upon Parliament the seriousness of the situation, the Government suggested that a Mixed Military Commission be created to study Belgian defense needs. The Commission came into being by royal decree on March 25 (two weeks after the Rhineland reoccupation) and met thirty-seven times. While there was difference of opinion about application, there was unanimity on general principles, and the Commission called for immediate action on the purchase of matériel, antiaircraft defense, fortifications, and conscription. The Commission made it clear that Belgium was not totally unprepared militarily, but her strength was inadequate in the event that the nation found it necessary to rely exclusively upon its own resources.

By late summer of 1936 this likelihood had become an actuality. On March 9 Italy had annexed Ethiopia; on July 4 the League of Nations admitted that sanctions had failed and discontinued them; on July 16 civil war broke out in Spain, and on July 24 Germany extended the draft to two years. France and Britain still continued to drift, and Belgium, their reluctant partner, witnessed an outbreak of the historic national fear: that Belgian blood would soak Belgian soil for causes which had little to do with Belgium. It was imperative, therefore, that the Government adopt the program suggested by the Commission. While the Government realized that, in the event of war, the strength of the Belgian army would probably have little influence on the direction in which the war would move, it realized, too, that weakness toward a potential enemy was an encouragement to his aggression. But the adoption of this plan presented a dilemma. The project called for an increase in the period of conscription, yet the Flemings remained intractable, even in the face of national emergency, and refused to vote funds for military expansion so long as the international commitments under Locarno were outstanding.

The Commission had observed in its report that public opinion in Flanders—the workers as well as the *bourgeoisie* and the intellectuals—was hostile to any policy which would be based on that of France.[6] The Government had to choose: either to maintain the relationship with France and Britain and gamble on an eventual settlement of the Rhineland dispute, thus re-establishing Belgian security through international agreement, or to repudiate Locarno, creating her own defense behind the walls of non-involvement. The possibility of hedging the contingency and rearming at home while allowing France and Britain to pursue negotiations abroad was precluded by Flemish intransigence.

The Policy of Independence-Neutrality

The solution lay in a new foreign policy. Already in April, Paul-Henri Spaak, the Socialist foreign minister, had suggested this possibility to Parliament. "Belgian security cannot be achieved except by an immense military effort under a policy of independence, the only solution capable of realizing a perfect cohesion between Flemings and Walloons."[7] On July 20, at a banquet for the Foreign Press Corps, Spaak elaborated upon the reasons for a change in policy. The reality of European politics, he said, compelled him to forget completely his preferences for one or another political, economic, or social system. What he wanted was only one thing: "an exclusively and wholly Belgian foreign policy."[8] Belgium could no longer afford the luxury of preferences, nor could she be expected to fulfill international obligations which were now, through no fault of her own, beyond her capacity of support: "A people can only reasonably consent to war when its vital interests

[6] *Contribution,* p. 40.
[7] *Ibid.,* p. 40.
[8] *Ibid.,* p. 41.

are at stake, its independence, its territorial integrity, the defense of its liberties." [9]

Spaak did not reject Belgium's participation in the League or Locarno, however. He was compelled to limit his comments to observations about the inadequacies of both organizations without being able to present a policy which would be a substitute for either. As foreign minister he could make no public statement which would compromise Belgium internationally, but there was another reason that prompted his reticence. Within Belgium a second source of opposition had arisen against the military policy proposed by the Commission and supported by the Government. While the Flemish Catholics were opposed to military expansion unless Belgium's international commitments were dissolved (particularly Locarno), the internationalists in the Socialist party, on the other hand, were opposed to military expansion unless Belgium maintained her international obligations, particularly toward the League. On September 26, 1936, the Congress of the *Parti Ouvrier Belge* (the Socialist party) issued the following resolution:

> Deliberating about foreign policy, the Congress declares that it has never been and that it will never be a question of Belgium returning to neutrality . . . that its policy is and must be exclusive of all military alliance and within the framework of the League of Nations, a policy of complete independence without political, military, or economic restriction. . . .[10]

With this latest turn of events the Government's efforts reached an impasse. The two most powerful political units in Belgium were willing to sacrifice national security for such slogans as "hatred for France" and "internationalism."

On October 16 the King called a meeting of the Council of

[9] *Ibid.*, p. 41.
[10] *Ibid.*, p. 42.

Ministers with the intention of dramatizing the seriousness of Belgium's international position and of prompting the Government into action. Leopold listed the reasons why steps had to be taken: the rearmament of Germany, Italy, and Russia; the transformation in the ways of waging war, particularly the developments in aviation; the reoccupation of the Rhineland; and the breakdown in the workings of international security. He then presented a brief résumé of the report of the Mixed Military Commission and deplored the failure of the Government to act on its recommendations. He continued:

> Our military policy, like our foreign policy, which necessarily determines the former, should be offered not to prepare for a more or less victorious war following a coalition, but to keep war from our land. . . .
>
> Our geographic position commands us to maintain a military apparatus of sufficient size to dissuade any of our neighbors from using our territory to attack another state. In carrying out this mission Belgium co-operates eminently in achieving peace in western Europe, and she creates for herself a right to the respect and to the eventual aid of all states which have an interest in peace. . . .
>
> But our engagements should not go beyond that. All unilateral policy weakens our international position and rightly or wrongly stirs up trouble at home. Even an exclusively defensive policy would not achieve its aim, because irrespective of how prompt the aid of any ally it would only come after the shock of invasion which would be crushing. To battle against such shock we would be alone in any case. . . . It is for that reason that we must, as the Minister of Foreign Affairs said recently, follow a policy "exclusively and wholly Belgian." Such policy should aim resolutely at placing us beyond the conflicts of our neighbors. . . . I repeat, therefore, our policy has a unique objective, to preserve us from war from wherever it might come. And it is necessary that public opinion be indisputably assured of this. . . .[11]

[11] *Ibid.*, pp. 42–43.

At the conclusion of Leopold's speech, the Minister of Public Health, the veteran Socialist leader, Emile Vandervelde, asked the King in the name of the Cabinet that he allow his remarks to be made public. The request came as a surprise to Leopold, who nevertheless granted permission.[12] The words of the King thus became the policy of the Government, and on October 28 Parliament gave a massive vote of confidence to Van Zeeland.

Before accepting as its own policy the generalities of the King's proposals, the Government attempted to qualify them. The Senate's Committee on Foreign Affairs used the word "independence" to describe the new policy: "Belgium should practice an independent and autonomous policy, but she should not think of backing out of past commitments. She denounces no existing pacts, much less does she withdraw from the League of Nations."[13] In a speech which preceded the vote of confidence on October 28, Spaak declared: "I wish to repeat that our foreign policy does not mean a return to neutrality; we designate our foreign policy as one of independence."[14]

The limits of independence remained vague, however. The Government never spelled out how independence would differ in actual practice from neutrality, nor did it reconcile independence with Belgium's continued membership in the League and her outstanding obligations under Locarno.[15] Yet for all

---

[12] Meetings of the Council of Ministers are secret. They afford the monarch an opportunity to speak his mind on any topic without the necessity of ministerial approval. Thus Leopold was surprised when he received the Government's request.

[13] *Contribution*, p. 44.

[14] *Ibid.*, p. 44.

[15] In 1937 one of the sources of ambiguity was removed. On April 17, 1937, France and Great Britain officially sanctioned Belgium's policy of independence and issued a joint declaration, *not a treaty*, by which they relieved Belgium of her obligations under Locarno toward them, while maintaining their obligations toward her. Belgium agreed in turn to strengthen her armed forces, to defend her own territory in the event of aggression, and to close her territory as a freeway or as a base of operation for the troops of any aggressive nation. On October 13 of the same year, Germany gave a similar guarantee. The second source of ambiguity

its ambiguity the policy remained the basis of Belgian international life from the fall of 1936 until the war. At each crisis in European politics between 1936 and 1939, the Government reassured its nervous population of the wisdom and strength of its foreign policy, particularly its Socialist citizens who continued to distrust the virtues of independence. Spaak defended the Government's policy to a General Council of the Socialist party in February, 1938:

It [independence] is a policy which gives back to Belgium its traditional position. I believe that it plays an essential role in western Europe, essential to European equilibrium. We must have a position which will not constitute a danger for any of our neighbors. If we have alliances in the strict sense of the word we are no longer an element of peace; we become a cause of trouble. . . . I wish to say that independence is not a policy which follows the direction of others . . . nor is it a policy of isolation . . . nor is it a policy which gives us new friends at the expense of old; it is a policy which should be followed in such a manner that we are permitted to have good relations with all our neighbors. It is a policy which should abound to our credit.[16]

The following month Spaak told Parliament:

The policy of independence is not perhaps the ideal policy, but it is, I become more convinced each day, the best possible policy. . . . Faced with the debris of the Treaty of Locarno and the failure of the League of Nations, what should we have done? . . . It is necessary to keep in mind, above all preconceived theories, the indisputable facts: our geographic position, the relativity of our forces,

---

remained, however, and indeed was compounded by the stipulation of the Franco-British declaration that Belgium maintain her fidelity to the League of Nations.

[16] *Contribution*, p. 65.

the existence in our country of Flemings and Walloons; it is necessary above all to keep in mind that decisive element: in western Europe, Belgium is an essential factor of European equilibrium.[17]

On September 3, 1939, following the German invasion of Poland, Belgium declared herself neutral (the policy of independence had now become one of neutrality pure and simple), complying with the stipulations of the Franco-British and of the German declarations made in 1937. On October 7 Prime Minister Pierlot remarked to the press that nothing had yet obliged Belgium to take sides in the war and that she enjoyed a deserved peace:

> The position which we have taken today we assumed long before the events; it dates from 1936. It is not in contradiction with any former commitments since all the neighboring powers agreed to respect a neutrality which we expect to uphold. . . . Peace is the fruit of political wisdom and also of years of military preparedness.[18]

The Government's Defense of Independence-Neutrality

On December 19, 1939, following the first war scare in western Europe, in Holland, Spaak sought to quiet the fears of Parliament: "It suffices for me to repeat here with force that Belgium is neutral and intends to stay that way so long as her independence, the integrity of her territory, and her vital interests are respected." [19]

During the parliamentary debates of April 16–17, 1940, a week following the German invasion of Norway and Denmark,

[17] *Ibid.*, p. 68.
[18] *Ibid.*, p. 100.
[19] *Ibid.*, p. 103.

with war only two weeks away for Belgium, Spaak continued to champion the logic of the policy of independence-neutrality:

> Probably like the rest of you, during the past months I have often thought about our foreign policy announced five years ago. Just the other evening I reread the various diplomatic acts which concern us and the declarations which accompanied them. And I arrived once more at the comforting conviction that our foreign policy has been perfectly loyal and clear, perfectly honest. Doubtless, few countries have so well defined their objectives, limited their commitments to those which they were sure of being able to support, and enlightened their neighbors regarding their intentions. With us there is neither abrupt change nor surprise; whatever happens, no one will be able to say that he was deceived by Belgium.[20]

Following Spaak's speech, the debate closed with an almost unanimous vote of reapproval of the policy of independence-neutrality: 131 for, two abstentions, three Communists against. "Never did foreign policy meet with such general approval in Belgium."[21]

Unhappily for Belgium the policy of independence-neutrality was not successful. It was too many things for too many people. It had one meaning for the Belgian government, another for the Belgian people, and yet another for Belgium's neighbors. The Government had adopted this course of conduct in order to allow Belgium to rearm. The Government hoped thereby to keep Belgium out of war but was prepared to fight if necessary. The Belgian people, despite the protestations of the Government, believed that the policy had made Belgium into another Switzerland. Belgium's former allies under Locarno, Britain, France, and Germany, had reluctantly acquiesced in

[20] *Ibid.*, p. 112.

[21] *Belgium, the Official Account of What Happened, 1939–1940* (London: Evans Bros., Ltd., 1941), p. 24. Hereafter referred to as *Belgium, the Official Account.*

the policy in 1937, but their sentiments toward it were hostile. After the war came, France and Britain accused Belgium of ingratitude and lack of faith. Independence-neutrality had balanced France and Great Britain on the same scale with Germany. Had Belgium forgotten 1914? Had she forgotten the years of peace between 1830 and 1914, years purchased by British and French guarantee? Germany, on the other hand, claimed that for all her neutrality, Belgian sympathy remained pro-Allied. From most points of view the policy miscarried. True enough, it had allowed Belgium to rearm, but it was a vain and costly effort. Belgium was crushed within eighteen days after the invasion. The French blamed Belgium for the subsequent fall of France, and the British came close to annihilation in Belgium because of what they considered Belgian duplicity.

Failure of such dimensions cannot go unatoned. Those who play a part in it must seek to dissociate themselves from its responsibility or suffer the consequences of their deeds. As we shall see in a later chapter the recriminations over the policy of independence-neutrality and the royal question became enmeshed, and the opponents of King Leopold sought to shift responsibility for the policy from the Government to the King. Between 1936 and 1940, those who had been dissatisfied with independence-neutrality had voiced the same accusations. Events following 1940 caused the statements answering these earlier charges to lose none of their vigor. On December 26, 1936, Prime Minister Van Zeeland had said before the House of Representatives:

> Someone has dared, from this tribune, to attempt to establish a distinction, how I don't know, between the attitude of the Government and the speech of the King. Has it been forgotten that the publication of the discourse was an act of the Government? We are a parliamentary regime, a constitutional monarchy. The King acts through the intermediary of his ministers, and it is the Government

which assumes responsibility, which endorses, which applies, and which makes its own the magnificent doctrine set forth in the royal speech.[22]

Two years later on March 16, 1938, Paul-Henri Spaak addressed the House of Representatives:

> Belgium practices a policy called the "policy of independence" which found its first complete expression in the speech given by the King to his ministers on October 14, 1936, a speech approved unanimously by them and published with the approval of all of them, a speech whose directive ideas have received many times the warmest approval of Parliament. It is therefore as absurd as it is inconvenient to pretend, as it is done in certain publications and in certain places, that there exists a personal policy of the King in opposition with that of the nation.[23]

And on December 19, 1939, Spaak, speaking once again to the lower house, had this to say about King Leopold, who was leaving for The Hague to discuss with Queen Wilhelmina the German threat to Holland:

> Let me say that under these circumstances it is not enough for me to cover the King constitutionally. It is necessary that I thank him publicly for his magnificent efforts which for several years now have spared our country the horrors of war; for his wise counsel which he has never ceased to lavish upon the various governments which have succeeded one another; for the firmness of spirit with which he fulfills his difficult task; and for the example which he constantly offers to those of us who approach him, an example which brings forth respect, admiration, and affection.[24]

[22] *Contribution,* p. 46.
[23] *Ibid.,* p. 68.
[24] *Ibid.,* pp. 104–5.

CHAPTER 3

THE EIGHTEEN-DAY
CAMPAIGN AND
THE SUMMER OF 1940

THE WINTER OF 1939–1940 did not allow Europe sufficient time to recover from the shock of Poland and arm herself against a new kind of warfare. Germany took Poland in September, 1939, after sixteen days of blitzkrieg, a violent surprise offensive carried out by mechanized ground forces preceded by saturation bombing and covered by mass fighter attack.[1] But Europe had barely settled down to what the French and the Belgians called the *drôle de guerre* ("phony war") when Germany used the same technique against Norway and Denmark in April, 1940, and on May 10, 1940, invaded Belgium.

For all her preparation, Belgium was helpless. Her defensive armor was inadequate, and her offensive armor was almost nonexistent. She had few tanks; she had few planes, and most of these were destroyed on the ground during the first hours of battle. The army of 650,000 regulars and 250,000 reserves (more than 10 per cent of the population) together with the armed forces of France and Great Britain, which came to Belgium's aid, fought well, but could not stop the Germans.

---

[1] Germany had conquered all of western Poland by September 16; the Russians invaded eastern Poland on September 17, and on May 29 the invaders signed a treaty dividing Poland between them.

The Battle

The German attack began at 4 A.M. on May 10, 1940. After meeting with Prime Minister Hubert Pierlot, Foreign Minister Paul-Henri Spaak, and Defense Minister, General Henri Denis, King Leopold left for his field headquarters at Breendonk, near Antwerp. Following a tradition begun by the first Belgian monarch, Leopold I, and continued by Albert during World War I, Leopold III assumed personal command of his army.[2]

Shortly after the attack, the Belgian government called for the aid of Britain and France, basing its claim for assistance on the agreement of April, 1937.[3] The Belgian plan, in the event of German aggression, allowed three days for the Allied armies to take up their positions in Belgium along the fortified K-W line, which ran from Koningshoyckt (near Antwerp) in the north to Wavre in the south. The Belgian High Command considered this their Maginot line and based their defensive strategy on its invulnerability.[4] The Belgians had never con-

[2] Unlike his father, however, Leopold did not appear before Parliament to announce his leavetaking. Irrespective of Leopold's apparent breach of duty, later in the day at the joint session of Parliament, Pierlot stated that the King should be where the fight had broken out. This appears to be sufficient evidence that the Government approved his behavior and weakens the case of those who accused the King of treachery. These accusers claim that Leopold had deliberately failed to appear before Parliament so that he would have to make no public statement derogatory of Germany, implying that his entire plan of action, including the conduct of the military campaign, had been carefully prearranged.

Perhaps Leopold considered it unnecessary to announce his leavetaking because he had taken command of the army on September 4, 1939, following the outbreak of war in Poland; with the outbreak of war in Belgium he moved this command into the field. Perhaps, too, he considered the element of time. The attack in 1914 had followed an ultimatum, between which two events King Albert had the opportunity to appear before Parliament. In 1940, the attack was sudden and unannounced.

[3] See Chapter 2, p. 41.

[4] This position, known as K-W from the names of the terminal points, consisted of a number of works disposed on several lines. They were protected in front by a continuous antitank barricade and by flooding,

sidered holding the Germans along the Dutch-German border; their strategy was to delay the invader long enough to allow the guarantors to assume position. The first days of the war went according to Belgian plan, accelerated, however, by the unsuspected strength of the Germans. As a result of this acceleration the Belgians held only two days, not three, in the area of the Albert Canal, and were forced to fall back to the K-W line on the evening of May 11. The British and French, nevertheless, had had sufficient time to take up their positions.

A description of the method of attack used against the first enemy objective in Belgium gives evidence of the quality of the aggressor's preparedness. The fort at Eben-Emael is located close to the juncture of the Meuse River and the Albert Canal, which joins Antwerp with Liége. Its artillery protected three bridges which crossed the canal at Vroenhoven, Veldwezelt, and Briedgen. The Germans took this vulnerable outpost by an expertly executed *coup de main* which landed troops transported by glider and camouflaged by predawn darkness on the roof of the fort. The raiders exploded the defensive armament of the fortification, entered the breaches created thereby, and destroyed the cannon which covered the bridges. This took place while other German troops, transported in the same manner, surprised the Belgian detachments guarding the three bridges and captured them from the rear. Part of the German army, waiting immediately across the border in Holland, then moved easily into Belgium. This was diversionary strategy, however; the bulk of the German military forces was deployed to the south, east of the Ardennes.

In spite of the fall of Eben-Emael and the loss of two bridges [the Belgians had recaptured the bridge at Briedgen] the Belgian army carried out the only *independent*

---

while antitank traps were set deep in the position. An underground telephone system and a planned road system completed the equipment of the position. (*Belgium, the Official Account,* Appendix 16, p. 99.)

mission for which it was responsible—it held on to the
Liége and Albert Canal position long enough to enable
the bulk of the Allied forces to occupy the Antwerp-
Namur-Givet [the K-W] line.[5]

As of May 12 the Belgian army ceased to operate as an independent unit. King Leopold placed his troops under the
command of French General Gamelin, who became the generalissimo of all the Allied forces fighting in Belgium and
France. Leopold was following the example of Albert, who
had subordinated himself to the French supreme commander
in 1914. This is significant for two reasons. The Belgian accusers of King Leopold claimed that he failed to maneuver his
troops to the exclusive advantage of Belgium; the Allies, on
the other hand, and particularly the French, blamed the collapse of France on Leopold's tactics.

The capitulation as a military act, however, lay in the logical
consequence of events which followed the fall of Sedan on
May 13.[6] The German assault began on the morning of the
13th when the German army east of the Ardennes moved
against the French 9th Army in the vicinity of Dinant, where
only advanced elements were in position. Later in the day the
main offensive was massed against the French 2nd Army at
Sedan. The city was abandoned by the French that same
afternoon at 5 o'clock. The drive of the Panzer divisions
thrown into the breach at Sedan threatened to surround all the
Allied troops in Belgium. The irresistible German movement
westward and northward began to wedge the Allies between

[5] *Ibid.*, p. 37.
[6] The French have claimed that the failure of the Belgians to hold the
Germans at Eben-Emael permitted the enemy forces to regroup in the
south. However, the troops which fought the 9th and the 2nd French
armies were not those which took part in the attack on the Albert Canal.
The French thought that the Ardennes in 1940 were still the same barrier
they constituted in 1914. Marshal Pétain had told the Senate Army Commission that the sector was not dangerous. But the Germans cut right
through the forest using fresh troops that had not been in combat in the
north.

the French border and Holland. Holland capitulated two days
later on May 15. That same day General Gamelin ordered the
abandonment of the K-W line and the withdrawal behind the
Schelde. This meant the surrender of Brussels, Louvain,
Lierre, Malines, Antwerp, Tirlemont, Wavre, and Namur—in
short, most of the major Belgian cities. Leopold immediately
saw the consequences of such strategy. The Allies were aban-
doning the only strongly fortified position in Belgium and re-
treating toward the sea, but unless the ports could be kept in
Allied hands, the fate of the armies was sealed. Leopold's
ministers urged him to retreat southward, toward France, so
that in the event of defeat in Belgium the Belgian armies
could be regrouped to continue the war in France. Such action
was impossible. Not only were the French and British armies
deployed between the Belgian troops and the French border,
but General Gamelin had ordered a westward retreat, and
Leopold received his directives from the French Generalissimo.

The Germans continued their enormous onrush toward the
sea. They attacked the British and Belgian units in central
Belgium, forcing their constant retreat westward, but the German's concentrated attack was in the south across northern
France. From May 15 to May 20 they moved closer and closer
to the coast. On the 18th Péronne fell; on the 20th Cambrai;
on the 21st the Germans entered Amiens and Montreuil and
Abbeville. On the 19th, in the north, Walcheren Island lying
in the mouth of the Schelde fell to the Germans. It had been
held by Dutch troops and remnants of the French 7th Army
that had gone into Holland on May 10. The pincer was now
established. On May 19 General Weygand was recalled from
Syria to succeed General Gamelin as the commander-in-chief
of the Allied armies. On the 21st he called his first conference,
at Ypres. There he decided upon an offensive which would
restore the line near Arras and stop the torrent of Germans.
The offensive would move in two directions simultaneously:
the Allied armies north of the Germans would attack south-

ward, while the French armies south of the Germans would attack northward.[7] The Belgians had no weapons for such an offensive, so it was agreed that the British and French would carry the offensive while the Belgians covered them defensively to the north, extending their front over ninety kilometers in order to do so.

The British and French in Belgium, attempting to re-establish contact with the French armies on the Somme, threw the bulk of their forces in the direction of Arras, but by May 23 the Weygand offensive had collapsed. In the meantime, the Germans were directing their destruction at the vulnerable Belgians—vulnerable not only from the east with the enemy relentlessly upon them, but vulnerable also from the west; for by the 23rd, the Belgians were no longer permitted by the Allied High Command to use the bases at Gravelines, Dunkirk, and Bourbourg along the North Sea. Only Ostend and Nieuport were left to them. They were compelled to move their reserves of food, ammunition, and fuel and to evacuate the injured along a single railroad line. Leopold informed the British to his right that the last hope for the Belgians was a counterattack northward by the British Expeditionary Forces. By that time, however, the British, after the failure of the Weygand offensive, had cut themselves off from the Belgians and had begun their retreat toward Dunkirk.[8]

The Germans squeezed tighter. Between the 26th and the

----

[7] When it was pointed out to General Weygand that Abbeville had already fallen, thus making a northward attack almost impossible, he proved to be ignorant of the fact.

[8] "Planning for the evacuation via Dunkirk was begun at G.H.Q. so far as I am aware, about the 21st of May. Thereafter, Gort never wavered; he remained steady as a rock and refused to be diverted from what he knew was the only right and proper course." Field Marshal K. G. Montgomery, the Viscount of Alamein, *The Memoirs* (Cleveland and New York: The World Publishing Co., 1958), p. 61.

Winston Churchill, in his speech to the House of Commons on June 4, 1940, claimed that the Belgian surrender exposed the British flank and means of retreat. In his second volume concerning World War II, *Their Finest Hour* (Boston: Houghton Mifflin, Co.), he states that already on May 25 Lord Gort had decided to abandon completely the Weygand

27th they broke the Belgian line at four places and began to suffocate the Belgians in an area of 1,700 square kilometers, into which three million people were massed—soldiers, local population, and refugees. Food was giving out; the army had long since lost its bread ovens and was forced to bake haphazardly on the march; the water supply had become contaminated, and cases of typhus had already been discovered. To seed chaos among the troops, the Germans dropped leaflets showing a map of the Allies hopelessly surrounded. The legend read: "Comrades: here is the situation. In any case the war is over for you. Your leaders are going to escape by airplane. Lay down your arms." [9] The tract was close enough to the truth to have its planned effect: panic and suspicion. Over two weeks of constant battle against what appeared to be an invincible enemy had almost destroyed Belgian morale. To counterbalance the German propaganda, Leopold issued an Order of the Day on the 25th which declared: "Officers and Soldiers, whatever happens, *my fate shall be yours.*" [10]

---

plan and, acting on his own initiative, had begun the retreat toward Dunkirk. On May 26, the British War Office approved his conduct.

Considering the sequence of events, it is not unreasonable to assume that Leopold thought he had been abandoned by the British. According to Churchill, the evacuation had already begun two days before Leopold's surrender, and plans for it had been made almost a week before, if we are prepared to accept the word of Field Marshal Montgomery.

Let us consider further this passage from Weygand's memoirs, *Rappelé au service:*

> On the 27th of May, the Belgian army found itself in a perilous situation. Its equipment was too far from the Yser to enable it to take position there in a reasonable length of time. Its right wing, threatened by encirclement, could no longer be freed by either the French or the English, whose evacuation toward Dunkirk had already begun. Without doubt, the Belgian command thought it had been abandoned by its Allies. That is how I judge today the decision on which time will bring the judgment of history.

[9] *Belgium, the Official Account,* Appendix 19, p. 102.

[10] *Recueil de documents établi par le Secrétariat du Roi concernant la période 1936–1949* (Bruxelles: Imprimerie et Publicité du Marais, n.d.), p. 47. Emphasis added. Hereafter cited as *Recueil.* This is a collection of

On May 28, the French Generalissimo ordered the Belgian army to retreat westward, from the river Lys to the Yser, but Leopold refused to comply.[11] To have obeyed would have resulted in a massacre; his soldiers would have had to abandon their heavy equipment and take defenselessly to roads already choked with civilians trying to avoid destruction. Those moving along the highways would have made helpless targets for the German planes which had been strafing continuously since the 25th.[12] Leopold chose instead to end the fighting and sent a plenipotentiary to the Germans at 5 P.M. on May 27. At 11 P.M. the terms were returned to him: "The Führer demands that arms be laid down unconditionally." [13] The fighting war ended at 4 A.M. on May 28.

At the time Leopold was accused by the Allies, but particularly by the French, of surrendering without notifying his guarantors. This charge was revived by his opponents in Belgium after 1945. They asserted that he had fought the war

---

official documents for the period 1936 to 1949. In addition to certain writings of King Leopold from 1936 to 1940, the collection contains all official documents, not only those coming from the King, but also those exchanged between the King and the Government, from May 10, 1940, to 1949. For those cases in which the King's version of the documents differs from that of the Government, both accounts are given. The collection includes all pertinent documents from the royal archives, the entirety of which were opened to the *Commission d'Information,* whose report was published in June, 1947. (See p. 132.) Jacques Pirenne, Leopold's private secretary, stated in the Preface to the *Recueil* that, in order not to unnecessarily implicate third parties, only those *private* papers from the *Maison du Roi* were included which were needed to clarify disputed issues and facts.

In the letter written to Gaston Eyskens, the prime minister at the time of publication of the *Recueil,* Pirenne explained that King Leopold considered it necessary to make public the collection in order to establish his position once and for all.

[11] This was part of the plan designed at Ypres by Weygand. It was to be put into effect in the event of the failure of the offensive.

[12] Even in 1960 Belgians speak about the weather during the eighteen days. The normally overcast Belgian sky had been cloudless since the morning of the invasion. The sky belonged exclusively to the Germans.

[13] *Belgium, the Official Account,* p. 51.

so that isolation in the northwest corner of Belgium was deliberate and surrender an inevitable consequence.[14]

[14] The defenders of King Leopold claim that the accusations made by the French were an attempt to cover their own desperate failure and lack of preparation. They blame Paul Reynaud for initiating the anti-Leopold propaganda, but they feel, too, that Winston Churchill is not without fault. On May 30 Churchill told the House of Commons that "I have no intention of suggesting to the House that we should attempt at this moment to pass judgment upon the action of the King of the Belgians in his capacity as Commander-in-Chief of the Belgian army." (Churchill, *Their Finest Hour,* p. 95.) On June 4, however, Churchill announced that new facts compelled him to speak. What makes his objectivity suspect was the attempt to throw the onus of the war itself on Belgium. "The King of the Belgians called for our aid. If the Head of State and his Government had not separated themselves from the Allies that had saved their country from death during the last war, if they had not taken refuge behind a neutrality whose fatality has been shown by history, the British and French armies, from the beginning, could have not only saved Belgium but perhaps Poland as well. However, at the last moment, when Belgium had been invaded, King Leopold called us to his aid and we responded to his belated appeal. . . . Suddenly, without previous consultation, with the shortest possible warning, without taking counsel with his Ministers, and on his own initiative, he sent a plenipotentiary to the German High Command, surrendered with his army and exposed our entire flank and all our means of retreat." (*Recueil,* p. 144.)

It appears that Churchill had completely forgotten the guarantee volunteered by England and France in April, 1937.

One cannot be sure of the influence that Reynaud had on Churchill's decision, but William Grisar, a major in the Belgian army, has testified to a conversation which he had with Lord Keyes, British liaison officer with Leopold III. Keyes recalled a conversation that he had had with Churchill during which the latter had received a telegram from the French Minister of Information. The telegram read: "At any price, prevent Admiral Keyes from defending King Leopold." (*Recueil,* p. 141.)

On May 28, Paul Reynaud, the French prime minister, addressed his nation by radio. "I must announce a serious event to the French people. . . . France can no longer depend upon the aid of the Belgian army. . . . It is that army which has just capitulated unconditionally, in the midst of battle, by order of its King, without warning his comrades-in-arms, French or English, opening the road to Dunkirk to the German divisions. It was just eighteen days ago that that same King who until then had affected to attach the same value to the word of Germany as to that of the Allies, asked for our help. . . . Then in the midst of battle, without warning General Blanchard, without regard, without a word for the French and British soldiers who answered his anguished call, King Leopold III of the Belgians lay down his arms. That is an event without precedent in history." (*Recueil,* p. 115.)

The brief account of the war given in the above paragraphs shows that the Germans commanded the direction of the war from the moment of invasion. The northwestward thrust was relentless, executed with skill and discipline. The Allied defeat was clear to those who cared to look.[15] Leopold told this to the French and British as early as May 20. He had already warned his ministers on the 15th that a final breach of the Allied front was probable and could easily lead to the isolation of the Belgian army and part of the British and French forces. Camille Gutt, the Belgian minister of finance, had warned the French Prime Minister, Paul Reynaud, when the former was in Paris on May 19. On May 20, Leopold, learning of the fall of Cambrai and the German threat to Abbeville, informed London of his concern. On the 24th, after the failure of the Weygand offensive, Gutt, this time in London, told Lord Halifax what measures should be taken to handle the critical situation in which the Belgian army found itself. After the separation of the ministers and Leopold on May 25, the ministers personally informed both London and Paris of what to expect. On May 26, the Belgian High Command warned General Weygand that the Belgian army had "nearly reached the limits of its endurance."[16] On the following day, the King sent a similar message to General Gort, the commander-in-chief of the British forces in Belgium.[17] Later in the day, the French liaison authorities were told that "Belgian resistance is at its last extremity; our front is about to break like a worn bowstring."[18] Before sending his envoys to the Germans at 5 P.M. on the 27th to ask the terms of surrender, King

[15] "Enough has been said to show that from the point of view of command and control of the forces available in France in May, 1940, the battle was almost lost before it began. The whole business was a complete dog's breakfast. Who must bear the chief blame? Obviously General Gamelin. He was the Supreme Commander, and, as such, was responsible." (Field Marshal Montgomery, *The Memoirs*, p. 54.)

[16] *Belgium, the Official Account*, p. 46.

[17] *Ibid.*, p. 48.

[18] *Ibid.*, p. 49.

Leopold informed both the British and the French missions.[19]

King Leopold did not deserve to be called a traitor for his surrender. The French Ambassador to Belgium, Albert Kammerer, in his book *La vérité en marche*, emphasized that the communiqués of General Weygand and Paul Reynaud revealed their full knowledge of Leopold's decisions.[20] Colonel Thierry, the head of the telephone communication service in the French army, in a statement to Jacques Pirenne, Leopold's private secretary, corroborated Kammerer.[21] Lt. Colonel Robert Duncan Brown, the military attaché to the American Embassy in Brussels in 1940, said that "in capitulating May 28, the King of the Belgians did the only thing he could do. Those who speak otherwise saw neither the battle nor the German air force." [22] Joseph G. Davis and Hugh Gibson, former American ambassadors to Belgium, William Philips, the American ambassador to Italy in 1940, and Herbert Hoover, without any doubt the American whom the Belgians most respect, all defended the behavior of the King.[23] Finally, Admiral Roger Keyes, in the Preface to Cammaerts' *The Prisoner at Laeken*, deplored the vindictive abuse heaped on Leopold, whom he considered the scapegoat for French failure: "I am glad to have this opportunity of declaring that King Leopold was steadfast in his loyalty to the Allies and did everything in his power to help their armies." [24]

[19] The French mission was able to warn Weygand in Paris, but General Blanchard, commanding the French forces in the field, could not be contacted, and General Gort could not be found.

[20] *Recueil*, p. 164.

[21] *Ibid.*, pp. 164–65. Statement made on January 17, 1943.

[22] *Ibid.*, p. 160.

[23] *Ibid.*, pp. 163–65. See Herbert Hoover, *Hoover Book, The Belgian Campaign and the Surrender of the Belgian Army* (New York: Belgian-American Educational Foundation, Inc., 1940).

[24] Cammaerts, *The Prisoner at Laeken*, Preface, p. vii. On May 10, 1940, Admiral Keyes, the British hero at Zeebrugge during World War I, was sent to Belgium as liaison between King Leopold and the British government. He remained until 10 P.M. on the night of May 27. He became one of the strongest defenders of the King and of his conduct during the eighteen-day campaign. His opinions, considered above reproach be-

The Separation of King and Government

Had the surrender been of military importance only, the controversy that grew into the royal question would have probably died away after the initial shock of defeat had worn off.[25] But the capitulation and its consequences had primarily political and constitutional significance, and the initial conflict between the King and his Government over military strategy, i.e., the Government's insistence that Leopold and the Belgian army retreat southward toward France and Leopold's refusal to consider such action, soon deepened into a controversy over political policy which led to the separation of King and Cabinet on May 25, 1940.

The capitulation and the events preceding it revealed the personality of the King more sharply than any series of events since his accession. Leopold was called upon to continue the tradition of the soldier-king. He hoped to be worthy of the memory of his father and secure a like place in the sentiments of his people. Possibly for the first time he felt free from what

---

cause of his reputation and war record, were quoted and requoted during the royal affair by the pro-Leopold faction.

[25] In May, 1940, the King's right to capitulate militarily was a debatable constitutional question. Article 68 of the Constitution makes the King the commander-in-chief of the armed forces. Leopold I, the first Belgian monarch, interpreted this as personal command and led his troops in the field. The tradition was continued by King Albert during World War I and by Leopold III in 1940. The Constitution does not specify, however, that this function is subject to ministerial approval. Leopold I was accompanied in the field by a responsible minister, and directives were issued in the name of King and Cabinet. Albert, on the other hand, although accompanied by his Prime Minister, who was also Minister of Defense, Baron de Broqueville, issued orders in his own name, leaving the impression that he alone made the final decisions regarding military strategy and policy. This impression was strengthened by Albert's statement made to Parliament at the first session following the war that he was returning to give account of his behavior. Parliament, by approving the results, victory, approved tacitly the means by which such victory was achieved.

he considered the fetters of his ministers, particularly remembering the strained relationship that had existed between him and his various governments since 1934 and his opinion of parliamentary procedure, which had grown out of it. The glamour of battle is often strong for an ordinary man; for a warrior-king it must have been irresistible. The power to command, the manipulating of human life: isn't this what kings are born for?

Those things which separate the prince from the people must have been uppermost in Leopold's mind. This could explain the chilled and formal attitude toward his ministers when they questioned the wisdom of his decisions. The eighteen-day campaign showed Leopold to be a man of courage and honor, but it showed him also to be stubborn and immature in the ways of a twentieth-century monarch.

King Leopold saw early the near-inevitability of defeat. The German blitzkrieg was unexpected. The precision of German military planning implemented by a war machine whose efficiency had no precedent could only be appreciated by those taking part physically in the battle. As a consequence, the Belgian ministers who met with the King during the course of the eighteen-day war accused him of defeatism when he predicted what could be expected; they later described his awesome clairvoyance regarding the disastrous progress of the war and its even more disastrous outcome. The mutual lack of understanding which resulted in the separation of Leopold and his ministers on May 25 began with the defeat at Sedan: the ministers were still convinced of the victory of the Allies; the King did not share their optimism. This statement must be qualified, however. The ministers believed that the Germans could be stopped by the Allied armies in the immediate future; King Leopold, on the other hand, believed that the Allies would win *eventually*, but he foresaw a war lasting ten or more years. At that time America was neutral, and the prospects of her entrance into the war were vague, while the Soviet Union had made its peace with Germany. The future for western Europe appeared hopeless. Leopold foresaw defeat and tried to salvage the most from it for his country.

For this decision, Leopold was called a traitor by his ministers. Though they soon recanted, an identification had been established which the King was never able to throw off. The ministers' accusation was reprehensible even considering their highly charged emotions during the days immediately following the separation on May 25. Militarily Leopold had acted with intelligence. But by surrendering his troops and refusing to follow his ministers into exile he acted unwisely politically, when one considers the relationship which should exist between a king and his ministers under a constitutional monarchy. Later on Leopold had to pay the price for the right to judge, to have an opinion; he had to pay the price for the lack of comprehension that blinded him to the limits of his authority, his obstinate inability to distinguish between his military and political capacities. His surrender of the army was not treachery, but his confusion as to whether he was surrendering his country and his permitting himself to be captured were the result of his limited political vision. In short, action taken with good intentions, i.e., the prevention of useless bloodletting, had political consequences which he should have foreseen. It is primarily this lack of foresight and its consequences which should be taken into consideration in judging the King.

The conflict between King Leopold and his ministers began on May 14, the day following the defeat at Sedan, as a difference of opinion over military operations. Prime Minister Pierlot urged the King to retreat southward toward France. Leopold answered that such orders would have to originate with his commanding officer, the Generalissimo of the Allied armies. It must be said in favor of the King that he saw the military conditions of the Allied armies more clearly than Pierlot, and his refusal to comply with the Prime Minister's demands was

logical and legitimate, for a southward retreat would only
have served to increase the probability of Belgian encirclement and defeat. The problems of surrender were discussed
at the next meeting between Leopold and his Government on
May 16. The King asked his ministers: "What has the Queen
of Holland done?" Spaak answered that she had gone to London with her Government and had issued the statement that
she intended to continue the war. Leopold replied: "Do you
think that she has acted wisely?" [26] Spaak commented that
from that Thursday (May 16) an uneasiness in regard to the
personal capitulation of the King began to grow in the minds
of the ministers.[27]

Following the meeting of May 16, Pierlot sent to the King
a written summary of the Government's position that allowed
no room for conflicting interpretation. He informed Leopold
that at all cost the King had to avoid capture:

> Regardless of the course of events and so long as the
> Allied powers continue the fight, the fact of the existence
> of Belgium must be affirmed by the continuation and the
> activity of the essential organs of state. . . . *The problem
> is not exclusively a military one. It does not concern solely
> the conduct of operations but also the political aspects of
> the war and all the consequences of the decisions which
> will be taken.*[28]

On May 20, Pierlot, Spaak, and Denis, accompanied this
time by Arthur Van der Poorten, the minister of the interior,
met with Leopold.[29] Afterward, the ministers composed a

[26] *Recueil*, p. 78.

[27] *Ibid.* These quotations and those given in footnotes 34 and 35 taken
from Spaak come from the address Spaak delivered to the Belgian legislators at Limoges on May 31, 1940. His speech was given extemporane-
ously; thus when he quoted others, his quotations were not verbatim but
from memory.

[28] *Recueil*, p. 67. Emphasis added.

[29] On May 16 the Government had moved from Brussels to Ostend; on
the 18th, most of the ministers had been sent into France; by the 20th,
the above-mentioned were the last four remaining in Belgium.

memorandum of the conversation and sent a copy to the King.
The ministers declared that the only policy they would sup-
port was one that required the King, in the event of defeat in
Belgium, to leave for France in order to continue the war.[30]
They rejected the conditions which Leopold had set down
during the meeting.[31]

Pierlot, Spaak, and Denis met once again with the King on
May 21, the last meeting before the separation on May 25.
The letter written by the King to Pierlot suggests what took
place:

> I do not think that I deserve the reproaches which the
> Government made against me of following a policy which
> would have as its object the conclusion of a separate peace
> with Germany. In accomplishing my constitutional mission
> as commander-in-chief, my primary concern has been to
> defend the country, while co-operating, as far as possible,
> in the war commanded by the Allied armies, and while
> seeking to avoid endangering our army. . . . The only dif-
> ference of viewpoint which has manifested itself between
> us is that in any case it cannot be a question of my sharing
> the fate of my army. I answered that it was impossible to
> exclude a possibility justifying that attitude.[32]

Pierlot answered the King's letter on the following day,
May 23:

> I have never kept from Your Majesty that I could not
> share his opinion concerning the extent of the constitu-
> tional provisions which grant to the sovereign the com-

[30] *Recueil*, pp. 68–69.

[31] Leopold had said that he would continue to fight: (1) if the Belgian
army remained in contact with the main French force; (2) if the French
and British continued to fight in spite of a Belgian defeat. He qualified
his readiness to leave, however, by the notice that if France and England
appeared that they would be compelled to make peace with Germany,
his place would be with his troops in Belgium. Leopold implied that *he*
would interpret *if* and *when* this contingency had arisen.

[32] *Recueil*, pp. 69–70.

mand of the army. That text does not depart from the general, absolute rule following which the government alone carries the responsibility for the acts of the Head of State. . . . In fact, the functioning of our institutions does not permit an accounting from anyone else except the ministers.[33]

Spaak commented to the legislators at Limoges on the anxieties of the ministers between May 21 and May 25 as they waited for the final decision of the King. He spoke of the terror which accompanied the ministers' realization that the King was going to accept a political role under the occupation:

> The King had a certain number of radically false ideas:
> 1) The Belgian army should fight only on Belgian soil.
> 2) The French and British Allies had been defeated and the war was over. Peace is going to be made and consequently it is necessary to change cards and seek, as far as possible, the favor of him who will be the victor.
> As I have said these are completely false, mistaken ideas. . . . We were aware of the reasons which the King wanted to take advantage of. We found them mad, stupid, more: criminal, because they indicated in the King a total collapse of a certain moral sense which shocked us.[34]

Answering the King's contention that Belgium owed nothing more to Britain and France, Spaak observed:

> Sire, you could have done something else had the country permitted you. You could have made a kind of isolated defense like the King of Denmark; you could have pretended. But you were bound from the moment that you allowed thousands of French and British soldiers to be called on our behalf and come be killed in the defense of

[33] *Ibid.*, pp. 70–72.
[34] *Ibid.*, pp. 87–88.

Belgium. If you abandon their cause, you will be a traitor and will be dishonored.[35]

By May 24 the ministers had decided to leave Belgium. They telephoned the King to determine his decision: either to follow them into exile or to stay, but he was not yet ready with an answer. The ministers, prepared to leave with a small entourage, went for a final interview which took place at the Chateau de Wynendael, near Bruges, where Leopold had transferred his headquarters. The following account of the interview, probably the single most dramatic episode in Belgian history, was written by Hubert Pierlot. It is too important and too fascinating not to be quoted at length.[36]

> PIERLOT: Many times already we have made known to the King our conviction that if the Belgian army were in whole or in part exposed to the imminent danger of surrender, the King should do everything possible to prevent his capture. We have told the King the reasons for this. The capitulation, which is perhaps only a military act, irrespective of how important the event, would of necessity take on a political complexion if the King were to sign it or if he were at the head of the army when it took place. Moreover, if the army must capitulate, the military role of the King would have finished, whereas he could continue to function as Head of State alongside the Allied governments. . . . This is the duty of the King. The Government unanimously shares this opinion. . . . As for the ministers, their presence near the King at the moment of an eventual capitulation could only contribute to the political aspect of the event which we would want to avoid at all costs.

[35] *Ibid.*, p. 89.
[36] The following account is taken from the *Contribution*, pp. 137–41. Pierlot wrote his account later from memory; there was no stenographic record of the Wynendael meeting. Only the King and four ministers were present—Pierlot, Spaak, Denis, and Van der Poorten. Therefore the quotations are not verbatim but reconstructed after the event.

The Prime Minister then explained to the King that the three other ministers would leave immediately and that he would remain until the last moment if only the King would agree to leave with him. Pierlot wrote:

> After a moment of silence, the King answered with visible effort: "I have decided to remain. Over and above the most substantial considerations from a logical or political point of view, there are reasons of sentiment which one cannot bypass. To abandon my army would be desertion."

Spaak then spoke to the King. (Until this point, the King had kept his ministers standing, indicating a short, formal meeting. Spaak asked that they be allowed to sit down since there was much more to be discussed. The King gave permission.)

> SPAAK: In the unanimous opinion of the Government, the King is going to make a serious mistake. By falling to the enemy he separates his cause from that of the Allies. He refuses to continue to fight at their side contrary to the moral obligations which he contracted in calling for their aid. . . . If the King remains, what does he wish to do? . . . Everything he attempts to do will compromise him and compromise the cause of our independence because the King will be acting under the control of the enemy. . . . I would like the King to give us some idea of the role to which he has alluded and which he will continue to play in Belgium.

> LEOPOLD: I do not know. I have no idea what it will be possible for me to do. But I hope to be able to continue to maintain a minimum economic life in the country and thereby to facilitate its provisioning and to spare my compatriots at least the worst sufferings, such as deportation.
> If I do not remain in Belgium I am convinced that I will never return. The Allied cause is lost. Within a short time, in a few days, perhaps, France in turn will be forced to give up the fight because the disproportionate strength [of

the enemy] does not permit her even the hope of success. Without doubt, Great Britain will continue the war—not on the continent, but on the sea and in her colonies. That war could be long. The intervention of Belgium would be useless, and as a consequence her role is finished. For a period which might last for many years Belgium will have perhaps limited independence, which will again permit her a certain national life while awaiting that day when, in the wake of unimaginable difficulties, more favorable circumstances will once again return for our country.

In these circumstances there is no longer a place for the attempt to continue the war alongside the Allies.

The decision which I am taking is terribly difficult for me. Certainly I would have an easier life if I retired to France, if I went to live there with my children, awaiting the end of the torment; but I believe that when two paths open themselves before you, the path of duty is always the more difficult. It is that which I have chosen.

THE MINISTERS: In the opinion of the King, what should we do?

LEOPOLD: Man to man I say to you clearly, do what you think fit, and if you reason that you must leave, I will not try to stop you.

SPAAK: We cannot be content with that answer from the King. We ask for instructions, but first we must make sure of the King's conception of the role which he will yet be called upon to play in Belgium. Will the King have a government?

Pierlot writes that before answering, the Sovereign reflected, and the expression on his face gave the impression that he had never asked himself that question.

LEOPOLD: Naturally, for I do not want to be a dictator.

SPAAK: Could that government, in the King's opinion, be the present one?

LEOPOLD: Doubtlessly not. It seems certain that the occupant would never consent to it.

PIERLOT: But if the King forms a government, what will be the position of the present Government, not only the ministers here present, but those who are in France? In the King's opinion, should they resign?

LEOPOLD: That appears to me in the logic of the situation.

SPAAK: It is necessary to foresee the reaction which will occur among the Belgians in free territory and to foresee the eventuality that the present Government, or another which might take its place, decides to continue the war alongside the Allies while . . . the King would have already made peace or would consider in any case that hostilities had ceased between Belgium and Germany.

PIERLOT: If the present Government takes the attitude indicated by Mr. Spaak and continues the war in France, will that Government still be the King's Government?

LEOPOLD: No, the Government would necessarily be opposed to me.

Pierlot again observed that the King's answers were always given concisely, but each time after a moment of reflection, which led the ministers to believe that the eventualities raised by them had not been previously considered by the Sovereign, or if they had, had not been given his thorough examination. The ministers then wondered if perhaps they should stay with the King in some unofficial capacity.

LEOPOLD: It would be advantageous to have as many persons as possible in Belgium having a moral authority which they could employ to maintain the cohesion and unity of the country. Moreover, even if the ministers resigned and were unable, as a consequence, to participate in the Government, couldn't they continue to aid me by giving advice and counsel which I might be led to ask of them?

The ministers were not long in rejecting this hybrid situation:

THE MINISTERS: Our place would no longer be with the King because, as we have already made clear, even if we resigned, our presence would help give to the events a political complexion which we wish to avoid or which we do not wish them to have by our act. Our place is with our colleagues with whom we could act as a unit once the Government were completely reconstituted.

Whatever they be, the intentions of the King, the conduct which he intends to follow, will be interpreted in Belgium and abroad, and particularly in the Allied countries, as treason to the cause to which the King and Belgium have been linked since they appealed for the guarantee of England and France. Far from being a rallying point, the King would occupy a contradictory position among his people. The monarchical institution, which has been the efficacious symbol and means of our national unity, would find itself compromised—without doubt, irremediably.

All attempts to persuade the King to reconsider his position proved futile. Before leaving the King, Pierlot said to him:

Following the letter and spirit of the Constitution, the ministers answer to all acts of the King either by formally assuming responsibility by countersignature or [by assuming responsibility] for public acts done by the Head of State in the exercise of his function. Since the creation of the Belgian state in its present form, all governments have considered that their essential duty has been to "cover" the Crown. None has ever failed in that obligation. In the present case we are forced to say that our attitude must be different. The King has adopted a line of conduct contrary to the unanimous advice of the Government; the latter has not ceased to voice its reservations. It would be too unjust to have weigh upon us a responsibility of which we should have to carry no part at all. It concerns a problem of extreme gravity upon which depends the existence of our institutions and of our country. We think that the King's manner of acting compromises everything. We have already said so. We do not want history to record us as the cause of the catastrophe which is about to take place. If the King persists in his intentions, we shall be forced not only to refuse to cover him but also publicly to break with him. We know that such a thing is without precedent and breaks with the traditions of public law. But we see no other attitude possible than that which we have just announced.

LEOPOLD: I understand your situation. You have a conviction. I know that it is sincere. You do as it tells you to do.

What began then as a dispute over military operations ended in a political conflict which went to the heart of the relationship between a king and his cabinet under a constitutional monarchy. The ministers had one policy, to continue the war alongside the Allies, beyond the borders of Belgium, while the King, it appeared, had formulated and intended to follow another. The ministers took their leave of Leopold fully convinced that he would treat with the Germans and continue to reign under enemy occupation.[37] This they considered to be unconstitutional because it would go counter to the advice of responsible ministers; Leopold, on the other hand, was concerned lest he fail to have a government with which to rule. To Leopold the presence or absence of a government in Belgium was the only significant factor in determining the constitutionality of his actions. The ministers believed that

[37] They left knowing, however, the following passage from the letter Leopold wrote to King George VI: "By remaining in my country, I realize full well that my position will be difficult, but my essential preoccupation will be to stop my compatriots from being obliged to be associated with any action against the countries which have aided Belgium in the fight." (*Recueil*, p. 131.)

the link of constitutionality would be broken from the moment of the separation.

After the surrender, the Government issued an official decree stating that the King no longer reigned:

In the name of the Belgian people, under Article 82 of the Constitution, considering that the King is under the power of the invader, the ministers united in council state that the King is found unable to reign [le roi se trouve dans l'impossibilité de régner].[38]

On May 31, those members of Parliament who had fled Belgium and were in France met with the Belgian Government-in-Exile at Limoges. The entire Cabinet was present with the exception of Antoine Delfosse. There were some present who wanted to vote a total repudiation of the king.[39] The leaders and in particular Pierlot had the discipline and good sense to remind the legislators, many of whom in the confusion and heat of recent events had lost perspective, that such action, even if possible, could only be taken by all the national representatives and not just by those present in Limoges. He was forced to remind them that the meeting at Limoges was not official and that the legislators could make no binding decisions.[40] As a result, debate was limited to a

[38] *Recueil*, p. 117.

[39] Others wanted to go even further. Mr. Buset was warmly applauded by certain members when he declared: "I accept nothing from the defenders of the King; I accept no extenuating circumstances. I say that the situation demanded of him a precise and imperative duty. He failed; let him be executed." (*Recueil*, p. 131.)

[40] The Government's declaration regarding the impossibility to reign was fully constitutional, however. In fact, the Council of Ministers now held both legislative and executive power. The king, under Article 27 of the Constitution, becomes sole legislator in the event that Parliament cannot act. Under Article 82, the Council of Ministers can assume the king's prerogatives under certain conditions. Those conditions were fulfilled as of May 28, 1940.

Pierlot, however, even considering his levelheadedness, was partly re-

statement of the repudiation of the capitulation and an interpretation of the words *"impossibilité de régner."* Many of the
legislators at Limoges felt that the words were equivocal and
failed to spell out the circumstances of this "impossibility."
Was it merely a physical impossibility or was it a moral and
legal one as well? The following resolution was voted unani-
mously by the members of Parliament:

> The Belgian senators and representatives present in
> France unanimously expressing their sentiments:
> Condemn the capitulation in which Leopold III took the
> initiative and for which he carries the responsibility before
> history;
> Bow with respect before those who have already fallen
> for the defense of our independence and render homage
> to the army, which has suffered an undeserved fate;
> Affirm their confidence in our youth which will soon re-
> place our colors on the battlefield;
> Declare themselves solidly behind the Government
> which has stated the *legal* and *moral* impossibility for Leo-
> pold to reign;
> Address to their compatriots in enemy-occupied Bel-

---

sponsible for the temperature of the debate on May 31. On May 28, he
had addressed the Belgian people by radio:
Ignoring the formal and unanimous opinion of the Government,
the King has just opened separate negotiations and has treated with
the enemy. Belgium will be horror-stricken, but the fault of one man
cannot be imputed to an entire nation. Our army has not deserved
the fate which he has caused it. (*Recueil,* p. 148.)

Pierlot had been infected by the venom in Paul Reynaud's attack on the
King and the army, and he feared for the safety of the Belgian refugees
in France, many of whom had been physically attacked by the French.
(See footnote 14.) This offers partial vindication, but the temper of the
meeting on May 31 had been strongly influenced by Pierlot's attitude only
three days before. It was abetted by Spaak's unique talent for echoing the
dominant tone of the moment. It was from his mouth that came the word
"treason." True enough, he was denying that there had been premeditation on the part of Leopold, but he labeled the King's actions as traitorous.
"When one speaks of this treason . . . the word burns my lips and chokes
me." (*Recueil,* p. 75.)

gium the expression of their warm and fraternal sympathy,
sure of their loyal patriotism;

Attest their firm resolution to consecrate all the forces
of the country and of the colony to the pursuit of the fight
against the invader until the liberation of Belgian soil,
alongside those powers which responded at the hour of
Belgium's attack;

Express their profound gratitude to France and Great
Britain which have fraternally opened their doors to the
refugees;

And affirm their unwavering confidence in the victory of
right and of honor.[41]

Between May 25 and May 28 the King changed his mind
about treating with the enemy.[42] His reasons are not known.
Some have said that the opinion of three jurists whom he
asked for advice, Albert Devèze, Joseph Pholien, and Hayoit
de Termicourt (respectively a minister, a senator, and the
attorney general of the Supreme Court), was decisive. Others
have said that Leopold had no other alternative. The Germans
did not offer terms; they demanded an unconditional surrender, implying that there would be no other government in
Belgium except the Government of occupation. Still others
believed that Leopold's failure to receive the requested countersignature forced him to realize that even from his own
point of view any future action on his part would be unconstitutional.

On June 2, Leopold asked his Government in Paris to send
an envoy to Switzerland to receive documents which would
clarify and vindicate the King's behavior from May 25 to
May 28. The Viscount Berryer met with the King's envoy,
Louis Frédéricq, who presented a copy of the pastoral letter

---

[41] *Recueil*, p. 138. Emphasis added.

[42] On May 26, the King got in touch with his ministers in Paris requesting a countersigning, a *carte blanche* approval, which would enable him to accept the resignation of his present Government and to
form a new cabinet. The request was rejected.

written by the Cardinal-Archbishop Van Roey informing the Belgian faithful that the King had not signed a treaty of peace, the text of a letter from the King to the Belgian diplomatic posts throughout the world, a duplicate of the Sovereign's last proclamation to his troops on May 25, a summary of military operations edited from the documents of the Belgian High Command, and the note signed by Devèze, Pholien, and de Termicourt.

The King's letter to the diplomatic posts, after giving a brief account of the war, the obstinate retreat, the encirclement, and the notification and prewarning to the Allies, concluded:

> The representatives sent to the German military authorities on the evening of the 27th had the precise and technical mission to inquire into the terms of a cessation of hostilities. The Germans demanded the unconditional deposit of arms to be accepted at 4 A.M. on the 28th. No negotiations of any sort were entered into. The English and French military missions assigned to the Belgian G.H.Q. were kept informed.[43]

The note of the three jurists was the most significant of the documents.[44] Part One concerned the circumstances leading to the laying down of arms and reiterated what is already known to us. In Part Two, the jurists took the position that by remaining with his soldiers, Leopold prevented a complete collapse of morale and insured them of better treatment by the victors. Concerning the legal aspects of the surrender, the jurists had this to say in Part Three:

> Contrary to what has been alleged, the King has not treated with the enemy; he has signed with the enemy neither treaty nor convention. The only order given was to lay down arms, a military order.

[43] *Recueil,* pp. 166–67.
[44] The entire note appears in the *Recueil,* pp. 167–69.

If the conclusion of a treaty or of a convention must be covered by the personal signature of a responsible minister, the same thing is not required for a military act or order. Without doubt, when the head of the army is able to keep in contact with his ministers, it behooves him to make no decision, even a military one, of primary importance without referring it to them or at least to one of them. But when all the ministers have left the country and communications with them have become impossible, the head of the general staff is invested with the power to decide, in conjunction with the King, all which concerns the military.

The order given in the manner it was could not possibly be subject to a constitutional objection even on the part of those who do not recognize the King's authority to decide alone, in his capacity as commander-in-chief of the army, all which concerns the military.

After finding that as prisoner of war the King was "temporarily unable to rule" the jurists came to the following conclusions:

1) The dramatic error which has consisted of accusing the King of having treated with the enemy and of having thereby violated his oath must be rectified immediately by all available means. The King has concluded no pact, treaty, or convention with the enemy; he has not acted except in his capacity as head of the army and in accord with the head of the general staff, after having decided that, all circumstances considered, any continuation of the battle by the army would lead to horrible consequences without any appreciable military usefulness. . . . On the 25th, in a poignant message to his army he sought to galvanize the troops by announcing to them that whatever happened their fate would be his. That admirable self-denial sustained their courage and thus prolonged the resistance. Everyone, officers and soldiers, dismayed by the errors committed abroad . . . have manifested their loyalty to

the Sovereign. The same applies to the civilian population, which has had the opportunity to express its sentiments.

2) One cannot deny that the situation thus created will result in a deep division, which cannot help but become worse, between the Belgians remaining in the country and those abroad. In addition, the enemy will find excellent encouragement for a policy which will divide Belgium, a division for which the presence of the King constitutes a most powerful obstacle, an obstacle which must not be weakened.

3) In conscience, we are of the opinion that in the higher interest of the country, and above all personal consideration, the truth should be re-established, the union of Belgians reformed, and the prestige of the King totally restored.

4) Concerning the administration of the country, the law of May 10, 1940, authorizes wide delegation of power. For the rest, the King being a prisoner of war, in principle the procedure of Article 82 of the Constitution should be applied.

After his meeting with Frédéricq, Berryer wrote a summary of the interview:

The primary concern of the *chef de cabinet* of the King was therefore to draw my attention to the error contained in the first sentence of Mr. Pierlot's statement of May 28 which accused His Majesty of having opened separate negotiations with the enemy.

I then asked Mr. Frédéricq if he could explain to me why the King asked to be covered by ministerial signature if he did not have a political act in mind.

The *chef de cabinet* thought he could explain this by the statement that the King had only asked to be covered by ministerial signature in the event of some indefinite and eventual act which he might be led to perform, being separated from his ministers. The King even foresaw that a general peace could lead him to take a political position as

Head of State while his ministers, finding themselves in France, in perhaps revolutionary or at least difficult circumstances, would neither be able to join him nor give him aid.[45]

The King's vindication appeared successful. On July 21, 1940, the date of the Belgian national holiday, Prime Minister Pierlot in an address at Vichy declared: "We ardently wish that the thought which dominates all Belgians be that of national union around the King."[46] On December 6, 1940, Spaak sent a note to all the Belgian diplomatic and consular agents throughout the world in which he reached, among others, these conclusions:

1) The capitulation of the army on May 28 was inevitable. The continuation of the fight would have led to personal sacrifices out of proportion to the military results then possible.

2) The King wished to share the fate of his soldiers and his people in order to maintain morale and to lessen their suffering.

3) The King, a prisoner of war, does not govern, does not perform any political acts.

6) The Government is forced by circumstances to act without being able to consult the King, but it does not act against the King. The attitude of the King, a prisoner, and that of the Government in England, are not contradictory and do not conflict.

7) All those who swore the oath of loyalty to the King should maintain their respect. Today that oath implies obedience to the Government.

8) A state of war still exists between Belgium and Germany.

12) The orders of the Government read: "For an independent Belgium, for a liberated King."[47]

[45] *Recueil*, p. 175.
[46] *Contribution*, p. 216.
[47] *Ibid.*, pp. 242–46. The Government was officially re-established in London on October 24, 1949.

At a conference held in London at Chatham House on February 14, 1941, Pierlot said:

> The Belgian army, during the first days of May, 1940, was with its back to the sea, isolated, practically surrounded and in such position that defeat was inevitable. That outcome was delayed from day to day, from hour to hour to the limit of all that was possible. The decision to stop the fight was only taken after repeated warnings to the commanders of the neighboring armies, without mentioning the information personally given to the Allied governments. . . . We knew that the King obeyed what he considered to be his duty. . . . True, we could not share his way of interpreting the national interest. . . . In actual fact, since the events that took place in May and in spite of the difficulties and the dangers of equivocal interpretation to which his presence in occupied Belgium could lead, the position of the King has remained clear and simple: the King is a prisoner of war; he has constantly refused to do anything which would contradict that state of affairs. He has refused to exercise his prerogatives as Sovereign under the control of the invader because that function must be free, otherwise it threatens to compromise the principle of national independence. The attitude of the King is a permanent protest against the *fait accompli*. That attitude is a symbol and source of encouragement; more and more it becomes the center of all Belgian resistance.[48]

On May 10, 1941, in a radio broadcast from London, Spaak told the Belgians to "close ranks around the prisoner-King. He personifies the battered Fatherland. Be as faithful to him as we here are."[49] In July, 1941, the Government-in-Exile in London published *Belgium, the Official Account of What Happened, 1939–1940*. The text concluded with a tribute to the King:

[48] J. Wullus-Rudiger, *Les origines internationales du drame belge de 1940* (Bruxelles: Editions Vanderlinden, 1950), p. 277.
[49] *Contribution*, p. 254.

As he had proclaimed in order to strengthen the courage of his soldiers at the height of the battle, its commander-in-chief has since linked up his future with that of the army. By his dignified attitude, in the captivity to which he has condemned himself . . . he has shown himself to be the incarnation of a people which will not accept servitude.[50]

On August 3, 1941, Spaak commented in a speech given in London:

Last year the King was in conflict with his Government; those Belgians who remained in Belgium were at loggerheads with those outside. All those clouds, all those misunderstandings have been dissipated. . . . Now justice has been rendered to the army and to the King and to the country.[51]

Spaak reiterated these sentiments in a private letter to Leopold written on November 21, 1941:

We admire the attitude of the King in occupied Belgium, and we know what comfort he must bring to his compatriots. We often think of Your Majesty, of his difficulties, of his burdens, of his painful isolation. . . . Our feelings for the King today are what they were before May 10, a respectful and loyal devotion. We trust that Your Majesty is confident in us.[52]

It seemed that at least by late 1941 unity had been restored between the Government and the King.

[50] *Belgium, the Official Account*, p. 52.
[51] Wullus-Rudiger, *Les origines internationales,* p. 278.
[52] *Ibid.*

The Government-in-Exile

In spite of the rapproachment of June 2, 1940, between the King and the Government-in-Exile, the two parties moved along entirely separate paths throughout the remaining war years. It appears that it was *after* the rapproachment that Leopold decided upon his "Policy of Laeken," [53] which some called open collaboration with the occupant and others more accurately called political opportunism. The meeting at Berne on June 2, 1940, seemed to have indicated that the King was willing to support the position of the Government which declared that Belgium was still at war with Germany and would continue to be so until the final victory of the Allies. But events after the fall of France and during the summer of 1940 caused the King to reconsider and to plan for the future in accordance with what he believed would be the greater good of his country. Contrary to his position stated to the Government's representative at Berne, Leopold no longer identified this good exclusively with the Allied cause; his policy by the autumn months of 1940 had been reshaped to make the most of victory irrespective of who eventually might win the war, i.e., either the Allied or the Axis powers.

Leopold's change of policy came about as a result of the confusion into which the Government-in-Exile was thrown by the fall of France. When the Government left Belgium on May 25, 1940, it did so in order that it might be able to continue the war alongside Belgium's allies, France and Britain. After the capitulation of Belgium on May 28 the Government-in-Exile, at that time in Paris, declared that the King was no longer able to reign and that the Government was assuming full executive authority.

[53] Laeken is the residence of the Belgian kings in the suburbs of Brussels. The official palace is in the heart of the city. It was at Laeken where Leopold was kept prisoner during the occupation.

On June 2, 1940, the British government recognized the Government-in-Exile as the only legitimate Belgian government. Surely this recognition was accorded by the British because they took the Government at its word that Belgium would fight with the Allies until the final victory. Yet, after the fall of France, the Government sought to treat with the Germans. The ministers later denied this, but denial could not remove evidence. On June 18 the Belgian government sent the following telegram to the Argentine minister at Berne:

The Belgian government, reunited at Bordeaux, requests the Argentine legation in Switzerland, through the intermediary of the Minister, Mr. Alberto Palacios Costa, personally to inform the Belgian Minister in Switzerland so that he might inform Brussels of the position which it [the Government-in-Exile] intends to take at the cessation of hostilities in France.

The Government states: (1) that it came to France in order to continue the war alongside of its guarantors; [It is significant that at this point, the Government failed to speak of Britain and France as "allies" but as "guarantors," the word Leopold had used all along.] (2) that the French army has stopped fighting; (3) that, under the circumstances, the Belgians in France should avoid any act of hostility against the Germans; (4) that the fate of the Belgian officers and soldiers should be identical to that of the French officers and soldiers; (5) that the civilian population and the refugees should scrupulously carry out the instructions which are given to them; (6) that the Government will resign as soon as the fate of the Belgian soldiers and refugees in France shall have been settled in order to facilitate probable peace negotiations between Germany and Belgium.[54]

On June 19 a similar message was sent to the Papal Nuncio in Switzerland, who forwarded it to Laeken through the Belgian

[54] *Recueil,* pp. 190–91.

Minister, the Comte d'Ursel. Then on June 26 the Government sent the Viscount Berryer, its envoy at the meeting with Frédéricq at Berne on June 2, to Laeken with a letter for Leopold from Prime Minister Pierlot, which included the following information:

> To sum up, we think that there are two urgent things to do: (1) to negotiate with the Germans the return of Belgian soldiers and civilians now found in France; and (2) to negotiate with the Germans the conditions of an armistice or of a convention concerning Belgium.
>
> Regarding the latter point, since we are badly informed, we wish to do nothing without receiving the advice of the King. If the King thinks that it would be useful and possible to form a new government, naturally we are ready to give our resignation.[55]

Other evidence also points to the Government's decision to resign. On June 18 it made arrangements for the governing of the Belgian Congo and Ruanda-Urundi for the duration of the war. It sent Albert De Vleeschauwer, the minister of colonies, to London, empowered to act officially in the name of the Government-in-Exile in matters concerning the Congo and Ruanda-Urundi. At that time, he was no longer considered to be a part of the Government-in-Exile, but was officially entitled "Administrator-General of the Belgian Congo and Ruanda-Urundi" with unique and sovereign power over these areas. One of the ministers, Marcel-Henri Jaspar, fell out with the Government over this decision and the general decision to end the war and went on his own to London hoping to rally the Belgians to continue the fight. On June 23 he spoke on the radio from London:

> The press agencies have announced that the Belgian government . . . has determined that it is necessary to

[55] *Ibid.*, p. 193.

end the war. That is false. The war will continue until the final victory. I have arrived in London with that end in view, and I await the ministers who want to join me. In the meantime, I shall continue the war. I am no one's prisoner. If necessary, I will exercise by myself the responsibility of power.[56]

On June 24, the Government-in-Exile repudiated Jaspar:

> Mr. Marcel-Henri Jaspar . . . has abandoned his post and his administration without warning his colleagues. He left for London for reasons of personal convenience. He was not charged with any mission by the Government. The Government absolutely disavows all statements made by Mr. Marcel-Henri Jaspar, whom his colleagues consider no longer a part of the Government.[57]

It appears that the Government seemed to have every intention of treating with the Germans and then resigning. Yet it did not do so. Again, as with Leopold's change of mind from May 25 to May 28 regarding his decision to treat with the invader, one cannot be sure of the Government's reasons. Spaak said in an address to Parliament in July, 1945, that between June 17 and June 25, 1940, the members of the Government changed their minds many, many times, one moment making plans to leave for England in order to continue to fight, the next moment ready to end it all. Although the Government denied it, perhaps Leopold's decision made known to Berryer on July 4, 1940, contributed to the Government's decision to continue the war: "The King's position has not changed. The King takes part in no political act and does not receive politicians." [58] On July 20, 1940, the German occupant in Belgium stated that it would not allow members of the

[56] *Contribution,* p. 204.
[57] *Ibid.*
[58] *Recueil,* p. 193.

exiled Government to return to their country. Perhaps this, too, encouraged the decision to carry on.

Whatever the reason for doing so, the Government-in-Exile established itself at Vichy in July, 1940, but it was able to prolong its existence for only a month. On August 1, the Bank of France refused henceforth to honor checks drawn by the Belgian government. Moreover, the Germans had ordered Pétain to end diplomatic relations with countries under Nazi occupation. As a consequence, on August 20, 1940, the Belgian government resigned and notified Leopold:

> The Belgian Government no longer has at its free disposal the funds belonging to the State which are indispensable to assure the payment of salary and provisions of the army and of the refugees. . . . In this situation, the ministers declare that it is impossible for them to fulfill their task and to continue the exercise of their functions. . . .
>
> Belgians: you will soon be reunited. You have known tragic times, submitting to the horrors of war and the miseries of exile. Our country, like each of us, has been deeply hurt. Do not lose courage or hope, however. Remain united around the King, symbol of an independent country. Long Live Belgium! [59]

The members of the Government separated. Some went to England; Pierlot and Spaak went to Spain with plans eventually to reach the United States. These plans miscarried, and in October they, too, were in London. On October 22, 1940, the Government-in-Exile was re-established in the British capital and remained there for the duration of the war. It was accepted as a full partner in the Allied camp and entered into international agreements which bound Belgium. The Government's most important international commitment resulted from the signing of the Washington Declaration on January 1, 1942,

[59] *Ibid.*, pp. 215–16.

which formed the wartime coalition against the Axis powers and which served as the first significant landmark in the evolution of the United Nations.

The Government contributed as much as it could to the Allied effort. At the end of October, it called into the armed forces all eligible Belgians in the United States and Canada and in all other countries not occupied by the enemy.[60] Belgians fought together in special units of the British armed forces. A *section belge* was created in the Royal Navy, and the warships placed under Belgian command were eventually to form the nucleus of a postwar Belgian navy. Though Belgium had disbanded its navy before the war, she did contribute thirty-four merchant ships to the Allied cause. The small Belgian air force had been destroyed either on the ground or during the invasion, but the air force personnel who managed to reach Britain was integrated into the R.A.F. in small units.

The Congo was administered by the Government in London. It contributed about 7,000,000 pounds sterling to the war effort during the first year alone, and its troops fought along with the British against the Italians in Africa.

In February, 1941, the Belgian government, through its special ambassador to the United States, Georges Theunis, moved to secure more funds by obtaining a writ of attachment from the Supreme Court of New York against $260,-000,000 worth of gold being held in the Federal Reserve Bank of New York for the Bank of France. The French government appealed the writ, but the appeal was denied on August 8, 1942, by the New York Court of Claims. The decision was upheld on October 10, 1942, by the New York Court of Appeals. As a result, the Government-in-Exile was assured funds for its operations during the war. The Belgians contended that $260,000,000 worth of Belgian gold sent to Paris before the

---

[60] After the war, Belgians who had ignored the call were prosecuted as draft dodgers. Among those sentenced was Walter Baels, the brother of the Princess de Réthy and the brother-in-law of King Leopold.

invasion of Belgium had been shipped to Dakar by the French authorities despite instructions from the Belgian government to transfer the funds from Bordeaux to London. Later on, the French, on German orders, returned the gold to France for delivery to Germany. After the war it was alleged by a Nazi diplomat on trial at Nuremberg that the Germans learned about the Belgian gold from King Leopold himself, who wanted its recovery. This was denied by the pro-Leopold forces, who stated that the "treasure" mentioned by the Germans referred not to the national gold but to part of the private fortune belonging to the Belgian royal family.

As has been shown above, the summer and fall months of 1940 were a confusing period for both King Leopold and the Government-in-Exile. The Government was surely within its rights to make whatever decisions it thought best, including resignation and capitulation. Leopold, on the other hand, believed that he was entitled to formulate and follow a policy he considered to be in the best interest of the country. In this he was unwittingly encouraged by the indecision and vacillation of the Government-in-Exile during the summer of 1940. It seemed to Leopold that it was up to him to act in the absence of a Government whose members seemed to be wandering all over western Europe. These two policies, the opportunistic Policy of Laeken and that of the Government-in-Exile wholeheartedly supporting the Allies, did not change during the war, and except for three occasions, there was no contact between Leopold and the Government until January, 1944.

CHAPTER 4

THE ROYAL QUESTION
TAKES SHAPE

Contacts between King and Government, 1940–1944

FROM JUNE 2, 1940, until early January, 1944, there was no
contact between King Leopold III and the Government-in-
Exile. The Policy of Laeken, which some claim was passive
withdrawal and others claim was active opportunism, called
for the King's silence.

On three occasions the Government attempted to break
through this reserve. The first contact was sought shortly after
the fall of France when it appeared that the Government was
planning to treat with the Germans. On June 26, 1940, Pierlot
sent the Viscount Berryer to Brussels to inform Leopold and
to ask his advice concerning the Government's intention to
open negotiations. The Viscount's mission was rebuffed by
Leopold's *chef de cabinet*, Louis Frédéricq, who told Berryer
that the King would receive no one associated with the Government-in-Exile.[1]

A second attempt was made late in 1941 when the Government got word to the King advising him to oppose openly the
deportation of Belgians to German forced labor camps. No
acknowledgment came from Laeken. Finally, toward the end

[1] See Chapter 3, p. 82.

of 1943 when Allied victory seemed sure, the Government began to prepare for its return home. It was necessary to reach an understanding with Leopold not only in regard to the conduct of the war after the liberation, but also concerning the behavior of the King and of his entourage during the occupation. On November 3, 1943, Pierlot, Spaak, Delfosse, and De Schrijver wrote a letter to Leopold. It was carried by Pierlot's brother-in-law, François De Kinder, who was dropped by parachute into Belgium. De Kinder took the letter to Cardinal Van Roey in Malines, who delivered it to the King in early January, 1944.

In the letter the ministers admitted that "after the dramatic events of the month of May, 1940," it would be difficult to resume personal contact; nevertheless, they expressed their devotion to the monarchy and to the King:

> For the good of Belgium we all wish that the King once again make use of his constitutional prerogatives as soon as the occupation has ended; but we also all believe that the best way to carry out this objective would be for the King to follow the respectful advice that we have permitted ourselves to give him.[2]

They advised that the King formally address the nation immediately after his liberation and inform his subjects: (1) that after the capitulation of the troops in Flanders, Belgium had never ceased to be at war with Germany and that she would continue the war, in accordance with the Washington Declaration of January 1, 1942, against Germany and Japan until the final victory; and that peace would be concluded with these powers and with Italy only in agreement with the United Nations; (2) that Belgium expected to participate in the political and economic reconstruction of the world in close co-operation with the Allies; (3) that just sanctions would be meted out to Belgians who had collaborated with the enemy; and (4) that

[2] *Recueil,* p. 501.

order would be re-established in Belgium on the foundation of respect for the Constitution and for public liberty.[3]

The King's answer did not reach London. De Kinder, who was carrying the reply, was captured by the Germans and shot. The letter would not have been considered a proper response, however, for it satisfied none of the Government's demands:

> The King has never ceased to consider it a duty to main-
> tain national independence. The King, following the ex-
> ample of his predecessors, has always maintained respect
> for the Constitution. He has never had intention of doing
> it harm. He sees its eventual revision only by the will of
> the people freely expressed. The alleged reports which
> tend to throw doubt on these points are completely ground-
> less, and whoever is circulating them is committing a crime
> against the dynasty and against Belgium. As for the rest,
> since May 28, 1940, the King has strictly maintained his
> position as prisoner of war in the hands of the enemy. He
> considers it in conformity with the dignity of the Crown
> and in the interests of the nation not to depart from this
> position either directly or indirectly.[4]

The King's Political Testament

At the time of the liberation of Brussels, September 3, 1944, the Government had received no further word from Leopold. On September 9, the day following the return of the ministers to the capital, Pierlot was presented with a memorandum written by the King on January 25, 1944, five months before his deportation to Germany on June 7.[5] The document con-

---

[3] *Ibid.*, pp. 500–1.
[4] *Ibid.*, pp. 501–2.
[5] There were two original copies of the Testament, one each in French and Flemish, which were given to the President of the *Cour de Cassa-tion*, Mr. Jamar, and to the Attorney-General of the *Cour de Cassation*,

tained the Sovereign's opinions regarding what he considered to be essential postwar problems. It contained, too, a rationalization of his conduct since May 25, 1940, and a demand that the Government apologize for its attitude toward the King, an apology which Leopold said must be made before the Government would be allowed to resume power. The ministers interpreted the memorandum, which came to be called Leopold's Political Testament, as his answer to the letter delivered in January by De Kinder. It is significant that the memorandum was addressed not to the Government-in-Exile but to those who would be holding interim power after the liberation. It is also significant that there was nowhere to be found even the suggestion of contrition. On the contrary, the Testament was a document written by a man convinced that his cause was just.

Leopold prefaced the main body of the document with these words:

> Without any real military power, my presence abroad would have had only a symbolic value; a few ministers sufficed for this. . . . At the moment when the Allies were crushed by overwhelming disaster and the enemy exalted by unprecedented military success, it was by sharing the adversity of my army and of my people that I affirmed the indissoluble union of the Dynasty and of the State and that I safeguarded the interests of the country *whatever the outcome of the war.*[6]

The memorandum contained eight sections. The first six dealt respectively with the *entente* between Flemings and

---

Mr. Cornil. Additional copies were given to Pirenne, Frédéricq, and to the Grand Marshal of the Court. The Testament was to be presented to whoever was in command at the time of liberation. The first person to be presented with the document was Field Marshal Montgomery, the liberator of Brussels.

[6] *Recueil,* pp. 502–3. Emphasis added.

Walloons, social reorganization, political reform,[7] educational reform, military reorganization, and the maintenance of order. Only the last two sections are important for the royal question. Section Seven was entitled: "The Necessary Reparations." In it Leopold recalled the days immediately following the capitulation (from May 28 to June 2, 1940) and alluded to the meeting at Limoges.

> Those accusations which, in an obstinate blindness, demeaned the honor of our soldiers and of their Commander-in-Chief, have caused Belgium incalculable harm which will be difficult to repair. One could search vainly throughout history for a similar example of a government gratuitously heaping opprobrium on its sovereign and on the national flag. The prestige of the Crown and the honor of the country are opposed to allowing the authors of these words to exercise any authority whatsoever in liberated Belgium until they have repudiated their error and made complete and solemn reparation.
>
> The nation would not understand or allow the Dynasty agreeing to act in concert with men who have inflicted an affront which the world witnessed with astonishment.[8]

Section Eight was entitled: "The Foreign and Colonial Policy of Belgium":

> As far as her international status, I demand in the name of the Constitution that Belgium be re-established in her complete independence and that she accept engagements or agreements—of no matter what kind—with other states only in full sovereignty and for ample consideration.

[7] He suggested the creation of a *Conseil d'Etat.* "The country has need of well-made laws and regulations; the citizens have the right to be protected against the arbitrariness possible from a government whose powers will become more extensive. Ministerial responsibility must cease to be an abstract principle fastened to a code; it is necessary that it become a legal reality restraining ministers whose errors would compromise the interests of the state." (*Recueil,* p. 503.)

[8] *Recueil,* p. 506.

I mean also that no threat be made to those ties which unite the colony with the motherland.

In addition, I recall that under the terms of the Constitution, a treaty is valid only if it bears the signature of the king.[9]

The Government's letter, dated November 3, 1943, and Leopold's Political Testament, form the keystone of the royal question. Before we examine their implications, however, let us recall certain facts. There had been no definitive interpretations of or amendments to Articles 63 and 64 since the adoption of the Constitution in 1831. Political reality in the form of an evolved concept of parliamentary government and ministerial responsibility, both resulting from universal suffrage and the growth of disciplined political parties, was no longer congruent with the letter of the Constitution. Yet evolution toward full ministerial responsibility had actually retrogressed between 1935 and 1940, that is, between the accession of Leopold III and the beginning of World War II. If this was not true in theory, it was true in practice. In short, Leopold had been politically active during the years preceding the war, an activity forced in part by the inability of the parliamentary system to cope with political and economic crises.[10]

Under Articles 63 and 64 a dispute between the monarch and the cabinet would be resolved in the following manner. If the monarch remained adamant in his refusal to consider an opinion of his government, the cabinet would offer its resignation. The Parliament would then be called upon to settle the dispute, or, if not Parliament, then upon its dissolution, the electorate. If Parliament repudiated the government, the king would emerge victorious; if, on the other hand, Parliament supported the government, the king would be repudiated. While legally he could not be forced to abdicate (Article 63 assures the inviolability of the person of the king),

[9] *Ibid.*, p. 507.
[10] See Chapters 1 and 2.

his effectiveness as monarch would cease, making voluntary abdication the only logical alternative.

On May 25 when the Government and the King separated, each thought it had legality on its side. Had circumstances been normal and Parliament been in session or been able to meet, the dispute would have been settled by the legislature. This was not the case, however. The Government proclaimed itself to be the sole executive power and determined that the capacity of the King as reigning monarch had come to an end. Its actions would be judged by Parliament when that body was next able to sit officially.[11]

In the letter written in November, 1943, and delivered in January, 1944, the Government presented its demands to Leopold. It asked him to repudiate those about him whose conduct during the occupation smacked, if not of collaboration, at least of opportunism. The Government did not revive the controversy over the capitulation. It did, however, ask Leopold to declare that he had never doubted the outcome of the conflict and to admit that Belgium and Germany had been at war since May 10, 1940, and still remained so.

What would have been accomplished if Leopold had agreed to the terms of the Government? First, it would have forced Leopold to repudiate the Policy of Laeken.[12] Second, by forc-

[11] It should be remembered that the session at Limoges on May 31, 1940, was not official. See Chapter 3, p. 70.

[12] After 1945 the defenders of King Leopold characterized the Policy of Laeken as one of passive withdrawal. The *Report* published by the commission instituted by the King to document his defense took this position. This interpretation appears faulty. The logic of his argument rests on the Policy's characterization as active opportunism, *attentisme*, a wait-and-see attitude designed to make the most of victory irrespective of who the victor would be. As of September, 1944, it appeared that Leopold intended to base the rationalization of his wartime behavior on this premise. These words in the Testament are significant: ". . . *I safeguarded the interest of the country whatever the outcome of the war.*" (*Recueil*, p. 503. Emphasis added.) Circumstances after Leopold's liberation forced him to change his tactics and base his defense on a policy of innocent withdrawal. We shall see in a later chapter how this defense forced a strained interpretation of facts and how logical the interpretation would have been had it been designed to accommodate *attentisme*.

ing Leopold's acquiescence, it would have established the supremacy of the cabinet, determining once and for all how future disputes between sovereign and cabinet would be settled.

Leopold refused to comply. He did more: he challenged the Government's position as of May 25, 1940. Thus Leopold pitted his entire concept of the proper conduct of the war and his behavior during the occupation against that of the Government. But by doing so, did he not deny the Government's claim as the sole executive and the Government's announcement of his inability to reign on May 28, 1940? Leopold thought not. He interpreted the Government's request for permission to enter into peace negotiations with the Germans in July, 1940, as the removal of the stigma of the moral inability to reign proclaimed at Limoges. In other words, he considered himself unable to reign only because of the fact of occupation, but insisted that he was still the sovereign. The final statement in the Testament attacked the very legality of the Government-in-Exile as the sole executive: "In addition, I would like to emphasize that under the terms of the Constitution, a treaty is valid only if it bears the signature of the king." [13] It would seem that Leopold attempted to make two points: first, that the Washington Declaration of January 1, 1942, had no legal basis because it lacked his signature; second, and much more important, he was implying that the Cabinet did not exercise exclusive executive authority, a claim which constituted a direct challenge to its legality.

By taking this position, Leopold wanted to restore the relationship which had existed between him and his Government on May 25, 1940. He wanted to force a choice between his policy and that of his Government. His strategy was clever. He had composed the Testament in January, 1944, five months before his deportation. He reasoned that at the time of the liberation he would be away from Belgium as a prisoner, while his people were free. His critics say he solicited his

[13] *Recueil,* p. 507.

own deportation in order to insure his absence. He knew that the most pressing problem facing Parliament would be the fate of the King. He knew, too, that the Government-in-Exile would be returning. It was essential, however, that the Government not resume power automatically. Leopold tried to achieve this in two ways. First, the Testament was addressed not to the Government-in-Exile, but to whoever would hold interim power. Second, he demanded that the Government apologize before being allowed to resume its authority. If the ministers apologized, such action would accomplish for the authority of the King what Leopold's agreement to the terms of the Government would have accomplished for the latter's authority. If the Government did not apologize, Parliament would have to give its verdict. Thus, Leopold awaited the vindication of his position.

Leopold's strategy failed. The Government accepted the challenge implicit in the Testament. Pierlot gave an account of the Government's actions since May 10, 1940, and asked Parliament to judge a stewardship justified by victory. On September 19, 1944, Parliament gave the Government an overwhelming vote of confidence. While sanctioning the Government's war policy, however, Parliament did not censure the Sovereign. The face-saving possibility of avowing the legislature's pronouncement was still open to Leopold when his liberation would free him for a decision. Until this could happen, Parliament elected Leopold's brother, Prince Charles, to act as Regent. The King was declared to be unable to reign as a result of enemy action.

Three factors explain Leopold's failure. First, the psychology of victory caused the laurels to be placed upon those who appeared never to have doubted Allied success. Second, Belgium had become a member of the United Nations. To have supported Leopold's *attentisme,* and to have countenanced his policy of national independence set forth in the Testament, would have meant a repudiation of those countries which had been responsible for Belgium's liberation, not only the original guarantors, but also the United States and the Soviet Union. Third, the extreme right-wing elements (the Flemish Nationalists and the Rexists) had been discredited by the outcome of the war. In September, 1944, Parliament leaned heavily to the Left, where the philosophy was opposed to a strong sovereign. These factors were exacerbated by the regional dichotomy. The Left drew its strength from Wallonia and Brussels, the Right from Flanders. The arguments for and against the King became infected with the elements of sectional animosity. To this was added the circumstance that Wallonia had, from the beginning, been sympathetic to the Allied cause, not because of its intrinsic justice but because "Allied" and "French" were synonymous terms. *Attentisme*, to the Walloon, was not a national policy; it was automatically pro-German because it was not pro-French.

The Government's strategy, on the other hand, had so far been successful. Following the analysis presented earlier, the only logical action left for Leopold would be abdication, if, at his liberation, he persisted in championing the Testament. After his liberation in May, 1945, however, Leopold did not recant and refused to follow the course of abdication suggested by the Government. The result of his refusal was the indictment presented to Parliament by Achille Van Acker on July 20, 1945. If we carry the above analysis to its logical conclusion, this indictment and the five-year controversy which followed were unavoidable. The King had lost the battle for his vindication and with it he had to abandon his conception of monarchical power. But he refused to accept defeat on the issue of the monarchy's role, and this intransigence led to his forced abdication.

It cannot be denied that Leopold had acted for the good of Belgium in the sense that he meliorated her treatment under occupation, yet he was now caught in a moral dilemma. He could have spared Belgium the years of anguish brought about by the royal question. He could have done so by sacrificing himself "for the greater good of Belgium"; in short, he could have abdicated in 1945. But his sacrifice would have been more than personal and would not have left untouched the royal prerogatives of his successors. He would have sacrificed an entire concept of kingship in which lay the privilege of weighing the good and the bad. By implementing this authority to its fullest and by abdicating he would have destroyed at the same time the right which had allowed him to make the decision.

The Battle Lines Form

As the Allied armies pushed deeper into Germany and as the time of Leopold's liberation approached, opinion in Belgium moved toward abdication. Within the country itself, sentiment was divided along religious, ethnic, and geographic lines. Generally speaking, the Flemings, the great majority of whom were Catholic, insisted upon Leopold's unconditional resumption of authority, while the Walloons and the people of *l'agglomération bruxelloise* (the Brussels metropolitan area) sought his abdication. In Parliament, on the other hand, the majority opinion was anti-Leopold. On February 12, 1945, Pierlot resigned as prime minister and was succeeded by Achille Van Acker, a Socialist, who created a new cabinet with ministers coming from the four major parties. Although there were six Catholic ministers out of a total of eighteen, the shift in premiership reflected the leftist bias in Parliament.[14] The anti-Leopold, Liberal-Socialist-Communist bloc outweighed the pro-Leopold Catholic Right.[15]

[14] Only one member of the war cabinet was a minister in the Van Acker Government—Paul-Henri Spaak, who remained as minister of foreign affairs.

[15] The composition of the legislature in 1939 was as follows:

Party	Chamber	Senate
Catholic	73	62
Socialist	64	61

During the first week of May, 1945, the political battle lines were formed.[16] Three out of the four major parties maintained these lines until the end of the royal affair. Only the Liberals changed from a policy which allowed the King personally to decide his fate to one which called for his *effacement* (a euphemism meaning abdication). The Socialist party and the Communist party demanded abdication. The Catholic party would settle for nothing less than full resumption of monarchical authority. The *Fédération Générale du Travail de Belgique,* which grouped the Socialist and Communist trade unionists, followed the direction of those parties. The *Confédération des Syndicats Chrétiens* voted with the Catholic party. The rank and file of the *Ligue Démocratique Belge,* the Catholic workers' association, which included Catholic trade unions, co-operatives, mutual societies, Catholic youth groups, and women's organizations, was split in its support for Leopold; but the official position of the organization was like that of the Catholic party.[17]

On May 7, 1945, King Leopold III was liberated by the American 7th Army; he was found at Strobl, east of Salzburg, in Austria. The following day, both Robert Gillon, the presi-

Liberal	33	25
Flemish Nationalists	17	12
Communist	9	3
Rexist	4	4
Independent	2	–

(Following the war, the extreme right-wing groups, the Rexists and the Flemish Nationalists, were outlawed.)

The source for this table is "The Belgian Crisis," *News From Belgium and the Belgian Congo,* Vol. V, No. 23 (July 21, 1945), 174.

[16] Public opposition to King Leopold had begun earlier, however. On May 26, 1945, the Minister of the Interior made a confidential report to Van Acker giving the origins of this opposition primarily among the Communists and the Walloon Separatists, extremist groups advocating either Walloon autonomy or annexation to France. (*Recueil,* pp. 546–61.)

[17] This phenomenon in the *Ligue* indicates that among working-class Catholics there was considerable opposition to King Leopold. This was due partly to the fear encouraged by Socialist propaganda that Leopold's return would bring in its wake a loss of many social and economic privileges for which the lower classes had struggled so bitterly.

dent of the Belgian Senate, and Franz Van Cauwelaert, the president of the House of Representatives, sent telegrams of official greeting to the King, but they received no acknowledgment from him. On May 9 a delegation including Prime Minister Van Acker and the Prince Regent left Brussels for Austria.[18] During the three days of conference with the King, Van Acker informed Leopold of the positions already taken by the most prominent political, labor, and ethnic groups. He added that the wartime resistance forces, which commanded great respect and affection among most Belgians, violently opposed him, and he stressed that the Sovereign's return would provoke serious national division. Nevertheless, the Prime Minister suggested to Leopold that, before making a decision, it would be advisable for him to consult other political personalities.

Leopold clearly saw the implication:

> In short, the ministers showed that the situation was very bad. They prefer that the King abdicate, but they do not dare take responsibility for it. They want the King to decide for himself. And so that no responsibility could be imputed to them, they suggested that the King seek the advice of others as well.[19]

On May 12 Leopold became sick. It is not unlikely that the illness was legitimate, but it is undeniable that it was convenient. Leopold wrote to his brother that his state of health prevented him from returning directly to Belgium.[20]

By June 5, 1945, the King was sufficiently recovered to summon Van Acker. It should be observed at this point that the Prime Minister was a clumsy politician. Even today there is

---

[18] The Socialist Prime Minister was accompanied by a Catholic, Communist, and Liberal minister in addition to Mr. Spaak, also a Socialist. The Prince took with him his private secretary, de Staercke, and Leopold's *chef de cabinet*, Louis Frédéricq.

[19] *Recueil*, p. 537.

[20] *Ibid.*, p. 538.

general agreement that his selection as premier was unfortunate. His conduct of the negotiations with Leopold was inept; his lack of finesse delayed them unreasonably and deepened the bitterness. Van Acker could not have avoided recognizing the dangerous game then being played between the Government and the King: the Government wanted to force Leopold's abdication without spelling it out in ten ugly letters, while the King obviously was maneuvering for time. Yet Van Acker, at the second meeting, while informing Leopold of the growing opposition to him not only within Belgium but also among Belgium's wartime Allies, added at the same time: "As for me, I'll go along with the King. If the King returns, I accept to continue my duties, but the Communists, the Socialists, and the Liberals, who form part of the Government, will resign." [21]

Because of Van Acker's ambiguous behavior, Leopold postponed his decision until the third meeting with the Prime Minister, June 14–15. It was decided between them that Leopold would return to Brussels on June 18. The King's itinerary was drawn up, and a speech from the throne as well as a radio address to his subjects was drafted by Leopold and approved by Van Acker.[22]

When the Prime Minister returned to Brussels on June 16 and announced these totally unexpected arrangements to his ministers, he forced the Government into an obvious but unavoidable course of action—resignation. In explaining its decision, the Cabinet stated in a joint communiqué:

> The Government does not want to take responsibility for the political events which will inevitably result in Belgium from the moment the King returns.
> Under these circumstances, it has submitted its resignation to the Regent specifying that it would be impossible

[21] *Ibid.*, p. 566. This was indeed an unusual statement considering that Mr. Van Acker himself was a Socialist.
[22] *Ibid.*, pp. 568–80.

for it to carry out current business from the moment the King returned to Belgium, current business including inevitably the maintenance of public order and political responsibility for the words of the King.

The Government insists most strongly that the King form a government before his return to Belgium.[23]

The Government, in order to carry out the strategy threatened by Van Acker's blunder, was forced to act in a manner considered by many to be unconstitutional. It refused to maintain order at home should the King return, and at the same time tried to make this return impossible. The King could not function without a government, yet the Government knew that he would be unable to form another. The Socialists and the Communists were committed to his abdication and would refuse to form part of a projected cabinet. The Liberals, who might have been persuaded to act favorably toward the King under their former policy of allowing him personally to decide his fate, on June 18 came out officially for *effacement*, or, in other words, abdication.[24] The Catholics were not strong enough to form a single-party, majority cabinet.[25]

In spite of these odds, Leopold worked to create a government, and from June 18 until July 7 met with politicians of every complexion, members of the bar, businessmen, the high clergy, educators, and members of the military. On June 22 he acknowledged the congratulatory telegrams which Gillon and Van Cauwelaert had sent to him on May 8, the day of his liberation. The failure of this belated attempt to court the legislature and the advice he received from those who had

[23] *Ibid.*, p. 581.

[24] *Ibid.*, p. 583. On this same day, June 18, the F.G.T.B. threatened a general strike if Leopold should return.

[25] Van Acker refused to attempt to form a government as he had promised the King on June 15. In a note to the King dated June 19, Van Acker counseled abdication. (*Recueil*, pp. 579–81.)

traveled to St. Wolfgang [26] forced the King to admit that he could not create a new government. Still he refused to abdicate.

Contact with the Government was resumed. From July 8 until July 14 the members of the Cabinet met with King Leopold. This time, however, the ministers threatened a parliamentary debate unless the King agreed to abdicate, a debate which would expose to the nation the nature of Leopold's war policy and his behavior during the occupation. On July 11 Leopold countered with the suggestion that a commission of three ministers be created to examine his record. He promised to open his dossiers to those whom the Government would designate. But the Government's mood was now beyond compromise. Abdication was the only solution it would accept. Leopold refused. After a meeting during the night of July 13–14 with his mother, Queen Elizabeth, and his brother, the Regent, King Leopold announced his decision in a letter written to the Regent on June 14:

> The Constitution proclaims that all power comes from the nation. The nation wishes that Parliament, which is the legal incarnation of national sovereignty, be re-elected every four years.
> The disequilibrium which circumstances have established between the Parliament and the nation does not permit me, at this moment, to discern the will of the country. Therefore, before making a definite decision, I shall wait until regular elections have re-established the harmony which should exist between the composition of the [Legislative] Houses and the political opinion of the people whom they reflect.
> I have decided to submit to the manifestation of national sovereignty in the manner prescribed by our institutions,

---

[26] On May 18, 1945, Leopold moved from Strobl to a villa on Lake St. Wolfgang in Austria.

but I must solemnly affirm that only the national will could lead me to lay down the great duty of King of the Belgians with which the nation has charged me. . . . In a mood of appeasement, I shall not return to the country until a national consultation [27] has taken place.[28]

Leopold displayed a bewildering tenacity. His Political Testament had forced Parliament to choose between him and the Government-in-Exile, yet when Parliament made known its decision, Leopold refused to consider it a legitimate expression of the national will. He chose to await the "voice of the people" before considering abdication. The Government, on the other hand, had been unable to force abdication. Both the approaches used against Leopold had failed. The indirect approach, used between May 9 and July 7, would have allowed the Sovereign to retreat honorably (from the Government's point of view), while the threat to expose him made between July 8 and 14 proved to be ineffective. As a consequence, on July 17, the Government took further steps to block the King.[29]

Article 82 of the Constitution reads: "If the King is found to be unable to reign, his ministers, after having decided upon this inability, immediately convoke the [two] Houses [of Parliament]. The guardianship and the Regency are provided for by the Houses sitting in joint session." [30] On May 28, 1940, the Government had determined that the King was unable to reign, but it could not obtain parliamentary approval because of the war. The declaration made on May 28 stated that the

[27] The French word *consultation* is difficult to translate in the context that Leopold used it, and I have simply rendered it throughout as consultation. *Consultation* does not have the force of either plebiscite or referendum; Leopold himself at one point said that the consultation was to be a means of investigating public opinion, not a referendum. A referendum would have been unconstitutional.

[28] *Recueil,* p. 607.

[29] On July 15 the Government resumed authority.

[30] *Textes exacts de la constitution belge, de la loi communale et de la loi provinciale* (Brussels: E. Guyot, 1948), p. 82.

King was unable to reign because of enemy action. On May 31, 1940, at Limoges, a moral inability was also found to have existed. On September 19, 1944, at the first meeting of Parliament following the liberation, the legislature approved the policy of the Government, including, *ipso facto*, the declarations concerning the King's inability to reign. On May 8, 1945, Leopold's liberation marked the end of the inability to reign because of the enemy. The King was free but did not return to Belgium because of ill health. On July 8, 1945, his health no longer barred his return, yet he was unable to do so because the Government resigned, and Leopold found it impossible to form a successor government.

By mid-July, 1945, the reasons for the "impossibility to reign" were hopelessly confused, and there were no provisions in the Constitution to aid in removing this confusion. The Constitution did not specify when an impossibility to reign would come to an end. Those who had drawn up the document in 1831 had not foreseen an occasion like the one that had taken place on May 25, 1940; they had only anticipated conditions of impossibility such as sickness or insanity or death.

On July 19, 1945, Parliament acted to interpret Article 82 and passed the following bill:

> Sole Article: Since application of Article 82 has been made, the King does not resume the exercise of his constitutional powers until after a deliberation of the Houses sitting in joint session stating that the impossibility has come to an end.[31]

Of the 137 legislators present, 99 voted "yes," six voted "no," and 32 abstained. The law was important not only because it solved an immediate problem, but also because it marked a step toward the solution of the larger problem epitomized

[31] *Ibid.*, p. 82.

by the royal question—the conflict between constitutional tradition and evolving custom. The pro-Leopold traditionalists who stood opposed to increased parliamentary authority argued that since the Constitution provided that the decision to create a Regency originated with the Government, the decision to dissolve the Regency should likewise be taken by the Government, irrespective of the necessity for parliamentary approval. Senator Orban (Catholic) commented during the parliamentary debate:

> This projected law will be unconstitutional if . . . it modifies . . . the terms of Article 82 of the Constitution. . . . If the constituent legislators had intended to submit to the declaration of the two deliberating assemblies the manner in which the impossibility to reign should come to an end, they would have said so.[32]

To this Spaak answered:

> Don't you find that there is a much greater guarantee and proof of our sincerity to say that that power which is given to us by the Constitution is [in turn] given by us to all of you by a law which interprets or rather executes Article 82 of the Constitution. . . .
> I am convinced that this is the true spirit of the Constitution. When there is doubt about the authority which exists between the several branches of power, it is for Parliament to decide, after all is said and done. That is the spirit of the constitutional and parliamentary monarchy to which we are loyal with all our hearts which is the only [spirit] to which we are loyal.[33]

[32] Marcel Vautier, "Droit constitutionnel. Lettres du roi. Article 82 de la constitution. Impossibilité de régner. Comment en déterminer la fin. Fin de la régence. Pouvoirs des chambres. Principes applicables." *Revue de l'administration et du droit administratif*, LXXXVII (1945), 185.
[33] *Ibid.*, p. 186.

The law passed on July 19 marked the constitutional limits beyond which Parliament could not move to prevent King Leopold's return, yet that which he represented remained to be destroyed. Consequently, Leopold himself had to be "exposed." On July 20, 1945, Prime Minister Van Acker opened the royal question to parliamentary debate.[34]

[34] The Catholic ministers resigned in protest against the law passed on July 19, 1945, and against the parliamentary debate which would be opened on July 20. Carton de Wiart, speaking for the Catholics, said in Parliament on July 17: "Gentlemen, faced with such an extraordinary and serious event, the Catholics, who yesterday were a part of the Government, have decided that they should offer their resignation, not wanting to accept the responsibility for or an association with a position which is manifestly unconstitutional. . . . We believe that the Catholic ministers could not in conscience associate themselves with a position . . . which appears to us clearly to be a threat to our constitutional principles. In effect, Article 68 of our charter proclaims that the person of the king is inviolable and that his ministers are responsible. By a paradox which is a bit monstrous, I do not hesitate to say it, the roles are being reversed." (*Contribution*, p. 419.)

In place of this solution, Carton de Wiart proposed in Parliament, in the name of the Catholic party, that a "national consultation" take place which would allow the people to express their opinion. It is interesting to observe that the Catholics, who declared that the Government's bill and the parliamentary debate were unconstitutional, proposed what was in effect a referendum, considered by their opponents to be unconstitutional under the provisions of the constitution.

On July 20, de Wiart's bill was referred to committee. The fate of this bill, which had no influence on the debate about to begin, will be considered in a later chapter.

CHAPTER 5

THE GOVERNMENT'S
CASE AGAINST LEOPOLD

Introduction

THE CASE AGAINST LEOPOLD was argued by his opponents during July, 1945. It was not meant to discredit him on constitutional grounds but to destroy him politically. The constitutional question raised by the Government's letter, dated November 3, 1943, and by the King's Political Testament, written on January 25, 1944, had been settled essentially when Parliament approved the policy of the Government-in-Exile on September 19, 1944. Before that date, the behavior of the King was neither constitutional nor unconstitutional; it was simply ambiguous. Had the Constitution been clear or had the modifications of the Constitution brought about by political usage been universally accepted, the royal question would never have arisen. One cannot say without qualification that under a constitutional monarchy the sovereign has no discretion. This may be true in Great Britain, in Holland, in Scandinavia, but it was not true in Belgium before September, 1944. The action of Parliament at that time decided *ex post facto* that Leopold had acted unconstitutionally. Leopold, however, refused to accept this decision, and protected by Article 63 of the Constitution, resisted the demands for his abdication.

By July, 1945, the Government had reached its constitutional limits in the conflict with Leopold. The only alternative left to the Government to force the King's submission to Parliament was political action that would establish his unfitness, or what the average Belgian would call his immorality. The Government's attack was camouflaged with constitutional arguments, but this could not disguise its real purpose. The Government's charge was simply this: King Leopold III had believed in a German victory and proceeded to act as if the war were over on May 28, 1940.

Leopold's defense, as will be shown in a later chapter, was a refutation of the charge—an item by item denial of the Government's indictments, each of which had been designed to elaborate and spell out the details of the basic accusation. The type of defense chosen was unfortunate, but one which could not have been avoided. The weight of evidence shows that Leopold did not believe that Germany would be victorious, but he did not refuse to consider the possibility. He thought that Belgium should prepare for this contingency and he acted accordingly. Belgium was occupied by the Germans and might continue to be for many years.[1] For Leopold the war was neither over nor continuing. This technicality seemed unimportant to him. What he knew was that no Belgian army continued to fight the Germans after May 28 and that his nation lay totally subjected to the occupant. Therefore, let the Government-in-Exile continue to say that Belgium was at war. If the Allies should be victorious, they could not say that Belgium had refused to fight. If, on the other hand, the Germans should win, they could not say that Leopold had been an active belligerent. In retrospect the King's policy came dis-

[1] These sentiments were expressed by Leopold to his ministers before the separation and also to Lord Keyes at their last meeting on May 27, 1940. (*Recueil*, pp. 57–58.) See also *Documents on German Foreign Policy, 1918–1945* (Washington, D.C.: U.S. Government Printing Office, 1957), Vol. 10, 125.

paragingly to be called *attentisme* ("wait and see" or "wait and profit").

Leopold did not arrive at this policy at once, nor did he do so with premeditation. Like the Government-in-Exile, the King, too, was confused in the months immediately following the fall of Belgium and the fall of France. From May 25 until June 2, 1940, it appeared that Leopold was going to form a government in occupied Belgium. It was the fear of this that prompted the statements made by the Government-in-Exile in Paris on May 28 and in Limoges on May 31, 1940. Yet Leopold did not do so. One cannot say why conclusively. As earlier chapters have shown, circumstances played an important role in his decision. As of June 2, 1940, it appeared that Leopold had accepted the fact that the war would continue; the meeting at Berne seemed to indicate this. But the summer of 1940 was chaotic for those who were entrusted with carrying on the war (the Government-in-Exile), and it was probably during these confused months of the Government's indecisiveness that Leopold decided upon his policy of *attentisme*.[2] His defense after 1945 would have been logical and consistent had it been geared to the defense of this policy, which could then have been justified as an alternative to the policy of the Government. But Leopold adopted a different kind of defense, one that maintained innocence in the face of the Government's accusation of complicity. His defense appeared weak, however, because he had not in fact maintained

[2] See Chapters 3 and 4 for the discussion of the period from May until October, 1940.

Perhaps Leopold's real mistake was his failure to change his policy of *attentisme* when victory for the Allies became certain: "But what is so terrible in the case of the King is that at no moment did we see take place in his mind a healthy return to the principles which he had espoused in 1940." (Speech delivered by Spaak to Parliament on July 25, 1945. *Recueil*, p. 656.)

This seems to add weight to the evidence that the policy of the King was one of "wait and see" and not one based on the belief that Germany would be victorious. Had he believed the latter, it would have been to his advantage to reverse his position and openly embrace the Allies when their victory seemed sure.

an attitude of strict political non-involvement. In the minds of many Belgians, this weakness was synonymous with guilt.

The parliamentary attack against King Leopold was made by Prime Minister Achille Van Acker on July 20, and by Foreign Minister Paul-Henri Spaak on July 24 and 25, 1945. Van Acker preferred the charges while Spaak created the climate of prejudice in which these charges could grow and mature. In the speech made on July 24, Spaak re-created the events between May 10 and May 31, 1940, and spoke of the apprehension of the ministers as they came to believe that Leopold would treat with the Germans and establish a government in occupied Belgium. He said that the charges made at Limoges on May 31, 1940, were perfectly reasonable considering the knowledge which the ministers had at that time. Spaak did not say, however, that the Government had made its peace with Leopold only three days later on June 2, and officially paid homage to him in the White Paper, published in London in 1941, entitled *Belgium, the Official Account of What Happened, 1939–1940.* In the light of past events, the speech painted an incorrect picture, but it succeeded in recharging the memories of duplicity and suspicion and in reinsinuating the allusion to treason.

The Charges

The charges concerned the following events or persons, all in turn related to the basic accusation that Leopold had believed in a German victory and had acted accordingly: (1) the King's entourage; (2) the note written on August 30, 1940, by Louis Frédéricq, Leopold's *chef de cabinet* to d'Ursel, the Belgian minister to Switzerland, and to Le Tellier, the Belgian ambassador to France; and the d'Ursel telegram sent in September, 1940; (3) the King's trip to Berchtesgaden in November, 1940; (4) the King's visit to Austria; (5) the congratulatory telegram to Hitler on his birthday and the telegram of condolence to the King of Italy at the death of Prince Amadeo, the Duke d'Aoste; (6) the King's deportation in June, 1944; and (7) the King's second marriage.

The entourage.—When the accusers of King Leopold spoke of his entourage, they referred primarily to two men, Leopold's private secretary, Count Capelle, and Henri De Man, the president of the Socialist party at the outbreak of the war, and later a confidant of the King.[3]

Leopold was judged guilty by association with De Man. De Man was a Socialist and a utopian idealist who believed that the power of money had corrupted every human institution and that the parliamentary form of government was the instrument of this corruption. He awaited the transformation that would rid society of both evils and restore a just social order founded on the dignity of human labor and secured by a long-lasting peace. De Man saw that there would be no peace in Europe until the conflicts between France and Germany were resolved, and he welcomed the Nazi movement as the means by which a new Europe would be established. He was not convinced that the movement would be the ultimate constructive force, but he was convinced that it would destroy the decayed old order.[4]

---

[3] When the war broke out, De Man was attached to the Defense Ministry for the direction of "L'Oeuvre Elizabeth," which included *Les Loisirs du Soldat,* a welfare organization working among members of the armed forces under the patronage of Queen Mother Elizabeth. He was at the same time a liaison officer with a section of the G.H.Q. On May 11, De Man asked the King to relieve him of this position so that he might work directly with the King. Leopold granted his request and placed him in charge of the safety and security of Queen Mother Elizabeth. De Man remained closely attached to the royal household and became a confidant of the King. It was he who aided Leopold in drafting the official correspondence which the King sent to the King of England, to the Pope, and to the President of the United States explaining the reasons for the capitulation. It was he, too, whom Leopold asked to head a new government should the Germans allow it under the occupation.

[4] Henri De Man, *Cavalier seul, 45 années de socialisme européen* (Genève: Editions du Cheval Ailé, 1948), *passim.*

De Man did not oppose the Germans when they invaded Belgium. On the contrary, he told the members of the Socialist party in a manifesto issued June 28, 1940:

> Do not think that it is necessary to resist the occupant. Accept the fact of his victory and try to learn from it the proper lessons in order to create the point of departure for new social progress. The war has brought about the collapse of the parliamentary regime and of capitalist plutocracy in the so-called democracies. . . . Prepare yourselves to enter the ranks of a movement of national resurrection.[5]

On February 16, 1941, he spoke at a conference in Brussels.

> Here in Belgium the power of the state was becoming weaker and weaker while, on the other hand, the power of money increased its strength from day to day. The origin of national socialism had its causes; that is impossible to deny. It has now replaced outworn things, but in an ultimate sense national socialism has still nothing to say.
>
> I am not a German nationalist, but a Belgian socialist, or, if you prefer, a national-socialist Belgian. . . . Socialism wants a social order in which labor is able to rule and in which the right to work can have value for everyone. Often that is not possible without an authoritarian state capable of destroying the force of money.
>
> The time of parliamentary government has passed. . . . Democracy is more than a parliamentary system. . . . The parliamentary system is only its bourgeois form. . . .
>
> The State must take on a new form. That form can only be authoritarian since that characteristic goes hand in hand with revolution. . . . After the war Europe will have a new form. That is why we admit the principle of order and of fulfillment in a unified Europe under an au-

[5] *Recueil*, pp. 343–44.

thoritarian system. But we should not ask that of the Germans. It is necessary that it come from Belgians.[6]

The Germans were not willing to accept even such mild criticism as De Man's. In 1942 he was expelled from Belgium and permitted to enter Switzerland, certainly a rather mild form of punishment if compared with the treatment meted out by Germany to those who truly opposed the Nazi regime. That De Man was distasteful to the German occupant did not preclude, then, the accusation made by Belgians that he was a traitor. Surely he was not a traitor like Staf De Clercq, the chief of the National Flemish Movement (the V.N.V.), who looked to the Nazis for the creation of an autonomous Flemish state, or like the leaders of the Walloon Separatists who hoped that the war would bring about either Walloon autonomy or the annexation of Wallonia to France.[7] These men were violently anti-Belgian by being either pro-Flemish or pro-Walloon. De Man was pro-Belgian, but his unique and personal "patriotism" called for the destruction of those institutions to which most of his compatriots were devoted. He was a traitor *sui generis*.

The attempt to distinguish among traitors has significance for this study. It is not unlikely that the idealism which propelled De Man was infectious. De Man, too, was driven by a concept of "the greater good of Belgium," a principle congenial to Leopold. The King's mind probably did not have the breadth or subtlety of De Man's, but it is not unreasonable to assume that Leopold's belief that Belgium might be able to derive some advantage from a German victory was nourished by his association with De Man.

The case against Capelle, and to a lesser degree against Frédéricq, rested on the evidence of letters written by them to Raymond De Becker, the pro-German editor-in-chief of *Le*

---

[6] *Ibid.*, pp. 346–47.
[7] *Ibid.*, pp. 350–60.

Soir [8] during the occupation, and by the association of Capelle with Robert Poulet, the editor of the pro-German newspaper *Nouveau Journal*. On January 9, 1941, Capelle wrote to De Becker:

> I had the honor of giving the King your message as well as the special edition of *Le Soir* dedicated to Belgian unity.
> His Majesty was touched by this homage and has requested me to thank you for it.[9]

On November 18 Frédéricq wrote to De Becker: "On his saint day you had the occasion to address to the King a message of loyalty and fidelity. I have the honor of being requested to express to you and to all those for whom you wrote the warm thanks of His Majesty." [10]

Many claim that Robert Poulet, through his newspaper *Nouveau Journal*, acted as spokesman for the Crown. As we shall see in a later chapter dealing with Leopold's defense, this charge was denied. After the war Poulet was condemned to death for collaboration, but no word came from Leopold on his behalf. Pleading for her husband's life, Mrs. Poulet wrote a letter to the King which gave strong evidence of the association between Poulet and Laeken:

> Sire, it is the wife of a writer unjustly condemned who writes to you. That writer was condemned for having sincerely expressed his thoughts. But as you well know, he would never have publicly expressed himself under the circumstances if he had not been convinced that the King approved his actions. At least twenty times during the twenty-seven months in which he wrote I saw my husband leave for a rendezvous which your secretary had arranged and return from it calm and reassured. "From the moment

---

[8] *Le Soir* is one of the leading Brussels newspapers. It was edited under the occupation by the collaborator De Becker.
[9] *Recueil*, p. 364.
[10] *Ibid.*

that I am in communion with the King's ideas, I am at ease," he told me each time, and he would then tell me the significant points which the important person designated by the King had made to him. . . . It is possible that in 1940–1943 you did not believe that you would have to go so far as to protect a journalist who never ceased being loyal to you. . . . It is not less true, and you have known it ever since then, that that journalist did not write one line without having your moral support. You should consider it an outrage . . . that a man is condemned as a traitor who was engaged in a continual exchange of views with your closest collaborator, who acted according to your instructions.[11]

The Frédéricq note and the d'Ursel telegram.—On August 30, 1940, Louis Frédéricq, Leopold's *chef de cabinet,* sent a note to Le Tellier, the Belgian ambassador to France, and to d'Ursel, the Belgian minister to Switzerland, which note was to be relayed to London to Albert De Vleeschauwer, the administrator-general of the Belgian Congo and Ruanda-Urundi.[12] The occasion of the message was the recent announcement by De Vleeschauwer that the raw materials and wealth of the Congo should be used for the exclusive advantage of the Allies, and that the Congo should participate in military actions with the Allies against the Italian forces in Africa. Frédéricq's message read:

> The documents given to Princess Joséphine Charlotte [Leopold's daughter] and to the Grand Marshal have arrived at their high destination. The documents revealed that Mr. De Vleeschauwer often speaks of Belgium's "word of honor" (*parole donnée*) in order to justify his actions. His opinion is false.

[11] Scintilla, "Le drame Poulet-Capelle," *Le Flambeau,* No. 4 (juillet-août, 1949), 379–83. Poulet's death sentence was eventually commuted and he was allowed to go into exile.
[12] See Chapter 3, p. 81.

Belgium, independent and neutral, contracted no alliance. She undertook vis-à-vis her guarantors only the defense of her territory against the invader. Her word did not go beyond this. Faithful to that word, the country fulfilled its obligations to the extreme limit of its strength. It accomplished all its duties vis-à-vis the guarantors.

The radio has announced that the colony proposes to engage in military operations. Attention is brought to the danger which would come from the example of engaging troops beyond the borders of the colony. Moreover, Belgium has never been at war with Italy. The repercussions of such action would be incalculable. The Congo, which has assumed no more obligations than did the mother country, should take military measures only if directly attacked.[13]

D'Ursel sent the following telegram to De Vleeschauwer based upon the information in the note from Frédéricq:

According to instructions, we must reject the thesis that an alliance with our guarantors links our fate to theirs. Our counteragreement did not pass beyond the agreement to defend our territory. The war ended for us on May 28. We must not risk dragging into the fight the colony which must observe an absolute neutrality. We have never been at war with Italy.[14]

The d'Ursel telegram was written by Count d'Ursel, the Belgian ambassador at Berne, to Belgian diplomatic posts throughout the world. It was dated September 6, 1940,[15] and was based upon information which the Count had received from Capelle:

[13] *Recueil*, pp. 390–91.
[14] *Ibid.*, p. 391.
[15] The date is significant because on August 20, 1940, the Government-in-Exile resigned and had not yet reorganized in London. In other words, this was the period when the Belgian diplomatic services abroad were receiving no directives either from Brussels or from the Government-in-Exile.

At the present time it is difficult to form a considered opinion concerning our future. The general impression is that our political independence can be re-established, at least in part; that is essential. The events of the recent past prove that it is very difficult for a small country to influence events, even when the Head of State is as loyal as ours.

We have never admitted the thesis of the Pierlot Government according to which an alliance exists between Belgium, France, and England. Those two countries were our guarantors who came to our aid in accordance with their promise. Our counteragreement was to defend our land, but there was never either a common cause or the promise to link our fate with theirs. . . . We cannot uphold in any way whatsoever the ministers who, now either in London or in Lisbon, continue a war which is opposed to our interests and loyalty.

It is particularly reprehensible to risk bringing the Congo into the war, as De Vleeschauwer is doing. We believe that our colony should observe strict neutrality. In business affairs she should maintain the principle of the open door and sell our products . . . to anyone who comes for delivery.

It would be desirable that you and your colleagues re-establish relations with the diplomatic representatives of Germany. In actual fact we are no longer at war with that country; we should be loyal and correct. Without having *cordial* relations with the representatives of the occupant, it is of common interest that the relations be *courteous*. They will establish the rightness of our policy and will permit us to furnish and receive information valuable to the country.[16]

Spaak commented in Parliament on July 25, 1945:

Of course, I do not pretend that the terms of the telegram were dictated by the King himself; for if the document is disturbing in its meaning, it is truly odious in its

[16] *Recueil*, pp. 399–400.

form. But I am convinced, knowing Count d'Ursel, that it was not he who took the initiative [to send the telegram].[17]

The trip to Berchtesgaden.—On November 19, 1940, the King met with Hitler at Berchtesgaden. Leopold has claimed that the Führer ordered him to Germany and that he went only to seek from the Chancellor an amelioration of the food situation in Belgium and the repatriation of Belgian troops. Leopold denied that the audience was politically significant. Van Acker, however, declared in his speech on July 20:

> To those who say that the King went to Berchtesgaden by order of the Führer, I answer that it is not so. The audience was solicited by the King; the trip was premeditated and prepared long in advance; the interview with Chancellor Hitler had political importance. It was the King's sister, Marie-José, the princess of Piedmont, who, at the request of the King, arranged the interview with the Führer. . . . The interview at Berchtesgaden did not have as its object, or in any case did not have as its sole object, the discussion of the fate of prisoners and the food situation.[18]

Van Acker recalled that Leopold, traveling to Berchtesgaden, was accorded full honors by the Germans, and that the meeting with Hitler, for which the King wore his formal dress uniform, lasted two hours, after which tea was served, implying a cordial atmosphere. Van Acker's evidence came primarily from the account of the interview written by Paul Schmidt, Hitler's interpreter.[19]

Schmidt wrote that after greeting each other, the King thanked the Führer for everything he had done for Belgium, particularly the repatriation of Belgian refugees caught in

[17] *Ibid.*, p. 651.

[18] *Ibid.*, pp. 617–18. Princess Marie-José had married Prince Umberto, heir to the Italian throne, in 1930. Many claim Hitler often heeded her suggestions.

[19] *Ibid.*, pp. 417–22.

France. He also thanked him for numerous personal attentions, among them the return of the royal children from Spain.[20] Leopold said that he had no personal requests to make of Hitler.

The Chancellor then asked Leopold what he thought of future relations between Germany and Belgium. The King answered that above all he would like to know Hitler's intentions regarding Belgium and inquired if the Führer would guarantee Belgian independence following the war. Hitler answered that Belgium would be part of the general reorganization of Europe that would include all those states which were in Germany's economic and political sphere. Belgium's independence, as far as her internal politics was concerned, would depend on how closely she aligned herself with Germany. According to Schmidt, Leopold then asked for some guarantees from Hitler regarding independence. He said that public opinion in Belgium was uneasy because Germany had made no announcement concerning Belgium's future, whereas England had broadcast by radio that Belgian independence would be respected at the end of the war. After a discussion of these issues the King and Hitler spoke of the food situation and of Belgian prisoners of war.

Hitler gave no specific answer to any of Leopold's questions. Regarding independence, the Führer said only that Belgium would occupy a certain place in the framework of economic and political co-operation with Germany, but that any declaration to the Belgian people concerning this would be considered a weakness. The Chancellor concluded the business part of the interview with the comment that Leopold had been wise to end the war when he did, thereby avoiding the complete annihilation of the Belgian army. He said, too, that it was good that Leopold had remained with his people, because the King of Norway and the Queen of Holland would certainly never

[20] The royal children had been taken from Belgium to France for safety. After the fall of France they were taken to Spain.

reascend their thrones. Hitler guaranteed Leopold that Germany would not touch the Belgian royal house.

Spaak commented in Parliament on July 25, 1945:

> I have certain scruples when I see the whole country rise up and demand . . . the punishment of . . . those people . . . who had the same idea [as King Leopold] that the war was over and that it was necessary for Belgium to have a place in the new Europe which was going to be dominated by Germany. . . . Yet . . . there are some who seem to find it quite natural that the King of the Belgians, in the midst of war, should go to Berchtesgaden to take part in political discussions . . . and when these discussions were over to take tea with the Führer. . . . Well, gentlemen, if a clerk of one of our departments, or if one of my directors-general—or even a simple employee— had done much less than that, an investigating committee would have condemned him without pity.
>
> Truly we do not have the right to have two weights and two measures, to strike down without pity the small and the weak and to show indulgence . . . when it concerns the first citizen of the land who goes to Berchtesgaden to take tea for two hours with the Führer.[21]

The telegrams of congratulation and condolence.—The accusers of King Leopold cite the following evidence that he courted not only the Germans but the Italians as well. On April 22, 1941, a telegram was received at Laeken. It came from a Dr. Meissner, a Nazi minister, addressed to Colonel Kiewitz, the King's gaoler: "The Führer requests that you thank the King for the greetings expressed by him on the occasion of his [Hitler's] birthday." [22] On March 7, 1942, Leopold sent a telegram to Rome, via Berlin, transmitted by the *chargé d'affaires* of the Italian embassy at Brussels: "His Majesty the King, Rome. I express to you my deepest sympathy

---

[21] *Recueil*, p. 657.
[22] *Contribution*, 253.

on the occasion of the death of Prince Amadeo, a great patriot and brilliant military chief. Leopold." [23]

Spaak observed:

> Did the King of England, during the war, telegraph the King of Italy when the Duke d'Aoste [Prince Amadeo] died? It is very indicative of a state of mind. Can you imagine a state of mind like that? Belgium was at war with Italy. Italy was allied with Germany. Italy could have done us great harm. The outcome of the war at that time could have depended upon her action. . . . It happened that the General-in-Chief of that Italian army, who not only fought the English but also the Belgians, died after having been taken prisoner. A telegram of condolence was then sent to his family in which the memory of that great citizen and brave head of the army was celebrated.
>
> Either that represents the total absence of a sense of reality or it demonstrates that they were getting deeper into a policy in which they were already deeply involved. One cannot be opposed frankly and fiercely to Italy when one is not opposed frankly and fiercely to Germany.[24]

The trips to Austria.—During the war the King traveled to Austria. His defenders say he went to consult a dentist. Van Acker commented:

> The King, a prisoner, left the Palace of Laeken on several occasions. We would have nothing to say if he had remained in Belgium or if he had attempted to reach an Allied country, which would have been even better. But we are obliged to state that he offended public opinion by voluntarily going to Austria, to Vienna and Salzburg, during the war, to a country at war with ours where he was the guest of one of the most notorious Nazis in Austria— Count Kuehn.[25]

[23] *Ibid.*, p. 277.
[24] *Recueil*, p. 658.
[25] *Ibid.*, p. 615.

The deportation.—The accusers of King Leopold claim that he solicited his deportation from Belgium to Germany in June, 1944. They based their charge on a document allegedly written by Van Straelen, director of the Royal Museum of Natural History, who had been asked by various patriotic groups to inquire of the Sovereign his intentions in the event of an Allied invasion of Europe. These groups urged Leopold's presence in Belgium at the liberation and suggested that he escape his captors and go into hiding in order to insure it. According to the Van Straelen document, the contents of which were communicated to the Government in London shortly before Leopold's deportation, the King refused. Van Acker, revealing publicly for the first time the contents of this document, told Parliament on July 20:

> During the conversation which he [the King] had with the person of whom I have just spoken [Van Straelen] the King made declarations which one could only classify as very disturbing. He thought: (1) that at the moment of landing and, in any case, at the moment of liberation, there would be a bloody reaction in Belgium; (2) that he did not want to be a part of it, preferring to be away from Belgium and to return when it was all over; (3) that he did not intend to be present at the moment of the Allied landing; (4) that he did not want to meet any member of the London government; (5) that his departure would have the advantage of leaving to others the responsibility of the moment; (6) that the choice of a Regent would pose so many problems that they would not hesitate to abandon his election and ask the King to return; (7) that the Allied command would not fail to interfere in everything and that he could not tolerate this interference if he were in Belgium; (8) that the American and English generals were brutal and clumsy; (9) that he desired not to be present when all the dirty linen was washed after the Germans left. . . .

If the King was not found in Brussels at the time of the

arrival of the Allies, it is not because he suffered deportation. It is because he accepted it voluntarily, if indeed he did not provoke it, in spite of the counsel and the pleadings which were heaped on him before June 6.[26]

The second marriage.—Leopold's marriage to Liliane Baels in September, 1941, is a microcosm of the royal question. The frenzy of reaction to it has calmed very little in the nineteen years that have passed. Today in Belgium the mere mention of Miss Baels, now the Princess de Réthy, can provoke a diatribe in which the ex-King is either damned or praised, depending on the geographic and political origins of the speaker.

The essence of the controversy over the marriage is constitutional, but the significance of it is political and psychological.[27] This part of the indictment against King Leopold touched the emotions and sentiments of the people more directly than any other charge, including that of treason, and the politicians intent on breaking the King took full advantage of this sensitivity. Van Acker's statement well illustrates this technique:

> It was during the war that the King decided to contract a new marriage. By doing so he chose the family of which he became a member.
>
> The marriage did immense harm to His Majesty. In the eyes of the people a king is not like other men. He is considered a superman. The pedestal upon which the King was placed was destroyed by the marriage. . . .

[26] *Ibid.*, p. 621.

[27] The unconstitutionality of the marriage is incontrovertible. There may have been ambiguities over the interpretation of the King's duty and prerogatives as commander-in-chief of the armed forces, but there can be no doubt that a marriage is a contract requiring ministerial approval under Article 64 of the Constitution. Moreover, Belgian law requires that religious marriages be preceded by a civil ceremony. The civil ceremony uniting Liliane and Leopold followed the religious service. Third, it was King Leopold himself who determined the morganatic quality of the union, a decision not to be made by the sovereign alone.

The legend has crumbled, and nothing remains. The nobleman is furious. The bourgeois is unhappy; in his selfishness he asks himself why the King did not marry *his* daughter; and the common man understands nothing at all of it. He finds that the King should have married someone from his own world.

The people do not accept such a marriage. They accept it in a film, in a novel, in some other country, or in a history book. Some day they might be proud that the King contracted such a marriage. But today it is an error. . . .

The attitude of the King during the war constitutes a bad example for our young people and for the generations to come.

At every level of Belgian society there are to be found those who by their resistance to the occupant and by their devotion to the cause of the country have given magnificent proof of our national vitality.

One should legitimately have been able to expect of the first citizen of Belgium, throughout the years of mourning and trial, to be the very incarnation of the sufferings endured by his people and of their will to oppose under all circumstances the demands of the enemy.[28]

There are many Belgians who believe that the royal affair would not have turned out so disastrously for Leopold had he not married Liliane Baels. (Observe that the statement is "had he not married Liliane Baels," rather than "had he not remarried.") They are convinced that irrespective of the constitutional and political involvements, a compromise could have been reached between the Government and the King, had it not been for presence of the Princess.

To understand the hatred that many Belgians feel for the Princess, one has to appreciate the affection that all Belgians had for Leopold's first wife, the Swedish Princess Astrid. The twenty-five years that have passed since her death have lessened none of this devotion. She is still remembered as the

[28] *Recueil*, pp. 615–16. Emphasis added.

Queen who shopped personally in the stores, walked her children in the public parks, visited the sick, gave generously of herself to charity. It was she who warmed the cool aloofness of Leopold toward his subjects and re-established the affection which had bound King Albert and his family so closely to the Belgians. Her death was a personal loss which the people shared with Leopold.[29]

The suffering Leopold became almost a symbol to his subjects, particularly after the fall of Belgium: a handsome young man suddenly made King by his beloved father's premature death, a widower accidently responsible for the death of an idolized wife, a father of three motherless children, a leader defeated in war, a hero imprisoned by the enemy.

Liliane Baels, a Flemish commoner, unwittingly destroyed the symbol and shattered the identification between the King and his subjects, particularly where this identification was most intense—among women. The author was told that after the announcement of the marriage was made in December, 1941, there was a perceptible drop in morale, especially among the women whose men were prisoners of war, and it was most noticeable in Wallonia, where the percentage of prisoners was higher than in Flanders.[30]

If this beginning of public life was not sufficiently inauspicious for the Princess, the animosity against her was increased by the knowledge that her father, the governor of West Flanders at the outbreak of war, had fled before the Germans and that her brother was accused of draft dodging for refusing to join the Belgian army after 1940.

This animosity, now a part of the Flemish-Walloon friction and of the volatile wartime *incivisme* issue, was strongest

[29] The Queen was killed instantly in an automobile accident near Küssnacht in Switzerland on August 29, 1935. Leopold was at the wheel of the car and was seriously injured.

[30] To spread discord among the Belgians and take advantage of the racial animosity, the Germans released a much larger number of Flemish than Walloon prisoners of war. This in itself seemed to suggest collaboration on the part of the Flemings, even though in the overwhelming percentage of cases this was untrue.

among the *bourgeoisie*. It would seem that in a stratified but essentially bourgeois society like the Belgian, where social mobility is possible but limited, the *arriviste* (it matters little whether Princess Liliane deserves this epithet; she is "considered" a *parvenue*) is condemned if the social leap is too conspicuous or too easy. To satisfy bourgeois mentality the move must be earned honorably and quietly. A beautiful and intelligent twenty-five-year-old bourgeois woman marrying a king would be automatically suspect.[31]

The Country Waits for the King's Defense

A year of feints and parries separated the Government's indictment and the initiation of the King's defense. Leopold used the occasion of his change of residence from Austria to Switzerland to address his subjects by radio. In the broadcast he condemned the attack made against him by Van Acker and Spaak, and stated his intention to await the verdict of the people before agreeing to abdicate: "The Belgian monarchy is founded on the common will of the citizens. Whatever that will may be, whatever may be the legal means by which it is expressed, I accept its verdict in advance." [32] In other words, Leopold maintained the position he had taken in the letter he wrote to the Prince Regent on July 14. The King also informed the Belgians that on July 14, 1945, he had offered to Van Acker and the Government the opportunity to consult the royal dossiers.

In a speech to the Senate on October 16 Van Acker com-

---

[31] The aristocracy, on the other hand, was much more tolerant of her, in a spirit of *noblesse oblige*.

[33] *Recueil*, p. 673. On October 1, 1945, Leopold, his family, and entourage moved from St. Wolfgang in Austria to the château *Le Reposoir* just outside Geneva, Switzerland. The broadcast was made the day before the move, September 30. It was not transmitted by Belgian radio stations, however, due perhaps to the disputed constitutionality of the speech. Leopold had not received ministerial approval for his address, and the Left considered it unconstitutional.

mented on the King's broadcast: "The King gives us to understand that he offered to open his dossiers to us. I find myself
forced categorically to deny that affirmation." [33] Van Acker's
denial brought a counterdenial from Leopold's secretary,
Jacques Pirenne.[34] His statement was corroborated by the
Minister of Justice in Van Acker's Cabinet, Du Bus de Warnaffe, who had been present when Leopold made his offer. The
Premier's attempt to silence the King had miscarried because
of de Warnaffe, and on November 6, 1945, Van Acker was
compelled to announce that the Government would consent to
publish a White Paper in which all information regarding the
royal question would be included, not only the Government's
documents but those of the King as well. Leopold refused the
Government's offer but countered with the suggestion that he
publish his own White Paper to appear simultaneously with
the Government's: "The King considers that it would be impossible for him to allow the Government to publish his dossier,
the Government having taken the position of accuser against
His Majesty." [35]

The issue hung fire until the dissolution of Parliament on
January 9, 1946, and the Government's announcement that
elections would take place on February 17. Leopold then reopened the controversy regarding a national consultation, a
device rejected by a committee in the House of Representatives
on October 17, 1945.[36] He proposed in a letter to the Government dated January 16, 1946, that a national consultation take
place following the elections between which two events he
and the Government would publish their dossiers.

[33] *Recueil*, p. 682.
[34] Capelle and Frédéricq had resigned in June, 1945. On August 8, 1945,
Leopold had established a secretariat in Brussels with Jacques Pirenne,
professor at the University of Brussels, as its head. He also appointed
Willy Weemaes as private secretary.
[35] *Recueil*, p. 702.
[36] On October 17, 1945, a committee acted upon the bill proposed by
Carton de Wiart on July 17, 1945, and rejected it. See Chapter 4,
p. 105.

Regenerated by the verdict of national sovereignty, the monarchy, whatever is left of it by then, will resume its constitutional role which has been too long restrained.

If the nation does not declare itself frankly in my favor, I shall abdicate.

If, on the other hand, the Belgians place their confidence in me, I will resume the exercise of my prerogatives.[37]

The Government rejected Leopold's proposal reminding him that it appeared to contradict his statements made in the letter to the Prince Regent on July 14 and in the message to the nation broadcast on September 30.

Parliament is the legal expression of the sovereign will of the nation. Contrary to what the antinational parties supposed before the war, there is not and there could not be an antipathy between the *legal country* and the *real country*. The King has accepted in advance the verdict of the common will of all citizens whatever may be the legal means by which it is expressed. Moreover, as the Constitution stipulates, Parliament, offspring of universal suffrage, will be the interpreter of that will. The House [of Representatives] has declared that the proposition which the King has brought up again was incompatible with the Constitution and with the parliamentary democracy which it organizes and guarantees.

[37] *Recueil*, p. 718. The last paragraph of the same letter gives further evidence of Leopold's familiar attitude that as a king he should be judged only in the light of what he had done for "the greater good of Belgium" and only in the light of what he (Leopold) conceived that "greater good" to be:

At the critical hours of my reign, of which there have been so many, I obeyed only my royal conscience. One cannot fail to recognize that Belgium, of all the countries which were submerged by the terrible tidal wave of 1940, has the most rapidly reconstituted her forces because she did not use them during the occupation in vain and fratricidal conflicts. One can discuss the question, from a constitutional point of view, to know if I had reason or not to remain among my people during the war. But one must recognize that my presence preserved their unity and kept them from many horrible miseries which other countries suffered.

The Government is not able to revise that judgment.

Your Majesty fears that if the solution of the royal question is carried over after the elections [and not followed by a popular consultation] the elections will threaten the principle of the monarchy.

The principle of the monarchy is not in question, and the monarchy has continued to exercise its constitutional function since the liberation. The Government declares solemnly that neither the principle of the monarchy nor that of the Dynasty is disputed or threatened and that they are not the stakes of any electoral battle. On the contrary, to have recourse after the elections to the consultation rejected by the House is to create a dangerous precedent for the monarchy, which risks becoming elective rather than [remaining] hereditary.[38]

Leopold, still maneuvering to strengthen his position, responded through his secretary, Pirenne, that the Government had misinterpreted his proposal. He did not intend that the consultation be a referendum but the means of investigating public opinion, a device consistent with Article 40 of the Constitution.[39] He restated his willingness to publish a White Paper to appear simultaneously with the one coming from the Government. The White Papers were to appear *after* the elections, however.[40] On February 7 the Council of Ministers agreed to Leopold's proposal.

The elections held on February 17, 1946, neither solved nor clarified the royal question, contrary to the expectations both of the Left, which hoped to entrench itself more deeply, and of Leopold, who awaited vindication. As a result of the elec-

[38] *Recueil*, pp. 720–21.

[39] Article 40 declares that each house of Parliament has the right to investigate.

[40] Leopold said that he chose to publish after the elections because he did not want the Paper to influence the outcome of the elections. It is more reasonable to assume that he hoped the elections would make the White Paper unnecessary, or, if not unnecessary, would alter the perspective of the documentation.

tions, the Left bloc in the House outnumbered the Catholic Right by seventeen votes, compared to thirty-three votes before the elections. Catholic gains in this election resulted from the disappearance of prewar fascist splinter parties. In the Senate the Left's twenty-seven-vote majority fell to a single vote.[41] The new Cabinet, formed after great difficulty on April 3, remained tripartite under the premiership of Van Acker.[42]

The results of the elections reopened the issue of the White Papers. The Government was reluctant to publish; Leopold, on the other hand, was more eager than ever. His defense was still pending. A national consultation would not be held, yet the elections had given him encouragement. Leopold decided to appoint his own commission to which he would open all but his private dossiers. On July 14, 1946, the King's official letter of invitation to form a commission was sent to the following nine men:

1. Gaétan Delacroix—President of the Order of Attorneys attached to the *Cour de Cassation.*

2. Léopold Devos—First president emeritus of the *Cour d'Appel* in Brussels, former president of the Faculty of Law at the Free University of Brussels, and honorary professor at the same university.

[41] Results of the February election:

	House	Senate
Catholic Social party (P.S.C.)	92	83
Socialist party (P.S.B.)	69	55
Liberal party (P.L.B.)	17	12
Communist party (P.C.B.)	23	17
U.D.B. (*Union Démocratique Belge*)	1	–

[42] The tripartite coalition governed only until July, 1946, when the Catholic ministers resigned because of their party's irreconcilable opposition to the Left over the royal question. A tripartite leftist government, Liberal, Socialist, and Communist, was formed first under Van Acker and then under Camille Huysmans, a Socialist. It governed until March, 1947, when the Communists withdrew in order to go into opposition.

3. Pierre Graux—Former president of the Order of Attorneys attached to the *Cour de Cassation* of Brussels, former president of the Faculty of Law at the University of Brussels, and honorary professor at the same university.

4. Charles Loiseau—First solicitor general emeritus of the *Cour d'Appel* at Liége.

5. René Marcq—Honorary president of the Administrative Council of the Free University of Brussels, professor at the same university, former president of the Order of Attorneys attached to the *Cour de Cassation*, and member of the Royal Academy of Belgium.

6. Jean Servais—Minister of state, honorary attorney general attached to the *Cour d'Appel*, honorary president of the Administrative Council of the Free University of Brussels, and professor at the same university.

7. Léon van der Essen—Secretary general of the Catholic University of Louvain, professor at that university, and member of the Flemish Royal Academy of Science, Letters and Fine Arts of Belgium.

8. V. van Hoestenberghe—Former senator, Bourgemester of Bruges, and former president of the Order of Attorneys attached to the Court at Bruges.

9. Monseigneur van Waeyenbergh—Rector-magnificent of the Catholic University of Louvain, and member of the Flemish Royal Academy of Science, Letters and Fine Arts of Belgium.

An examination of this list reveals the geographic and political distribution of the commissioners. There were representatives from Flanders and Wallonia as well as graduates of and professors at both the Free (i.e., nonsectarian) University of Brussels—the Alma Mater of Belgian Socialists, Liberals, and Communists—and the Catholic University of Louvain. All except two of Leopold's choices were attorneys and all had impeccable war records. The distribution reveals this phenomenon: that no body which aspired to carry on "objective" research dealing with a national question could fail to represent the ethnic, religious, linguistic, and political dichotomy in Belgium.

It was this Commission of Information which studied for a whole year the files made available to them by King Leopold. It published its final report on March 25, 1947.

CHAPTER 6

LEOPOLD'S DEFENSE:
THE REPORT
OF THE COMMISSION
OF INFORMATION

THE COMMISSION'S DEFENSE of Leopold's behavior since May 25, 1940, was based upon a constitutional interpretation of monarchical power which was the reverse of the position taken by the Government.[1] The Commission revealed its political philosophy when it defended the following opinions expressed by King Leopold in 1936:

A constitutional monarchy is based on the principle of a rigorous separation of power. It supposes alongside a Parliament which legislates and controls, an executive which governs. The executive power belongs to the king . . . who appoints and dismisses his ministers . . . who alone are responsible before Parliament.

Today while our Constitution remains unchanged, the executive power in fact has ceased to be distinct from the

[1] The defense was presented in the document entitled: *Report of the Commission of Information Instituted by His Majesty King Leopold III 14 July 1946* (Luxembourg: Imprimerie St. Paul, 1947). It will be referred to henceforth as the *Report*. The *Report* contained 150 pages of text, divided into thirteen chapters, and 270 pages of corroborative documentation.

legislative power. In reality, it belongs to the political parties whose ministers have become, throughout the past legislatures, their orderlies. . . . As the executive power has weakened, the role of the State continues to grow. Thus by a paradoxical contradiction, the more the State finds itself obliged to act, the less is it able to do so.

The first condition which imposes itself, that upon which depends . . . the fate of our regime, is the restoration of a truly responsible executive power in all its independence and capacity for action.[2]

The Commission also quoted from other speeches made by the King before the war and approved the ideas presented in them.[3] "These principles formulated by the King on the eve of the war are the testimony of an absolute respect for parliamentary and constitutional institutions."[4]

Given this point of view, the Commission naturally found that Leopold's behavior from May 25, 1940, until his deportation on June 6, 1944, fell within the range of the King's constitutional authority. Yet this behavior could not be "proved" to have been constitutional; it could only be shown as legitimate within the frame of constitutional reference defined by Leopold in terms like those quoted above. But this frame of reference had been challenged by the Government and rejected by Parliament on September 19, 1944. The Commission, in order to relieve itself of the impossible task of proving the constitutionality of the King's actions, simply denied that constitutionality was an issue and claimed that the dispute over the break between Leopold and the Cabinet in 1940 and the consequences of this act were not constitutional but political in nature, i.e., a dispute over alternative political policies. By doing this, the *Report* hoped to accomplish two objectives: to imply indirectly the constitutionality of the King's behavior,

[2] *Report*, pp. 21–22.
[3] See Chapter 1, pp. 25–29.
[4] *Report*, p. 23.

and to challenge the validity of Parliament's action on September 19, 1944. Since Leopold had already denied the representative character of Parliament on that date, the *Report* placed the royal question, so far as the King was concerned, where it had been before September, 1944. Under these circumstances, the royal question was still open to further parliamentary action.

The strategy was skillful, but the tactics used to carry it out proved to be the undoing of the defense. The *Report* considered Leopold's behavior exclusively a political question and asked the Belgian people to examine and judge a policy which the King had considered best for the country. That policy could only be defined as *attentisme*, yet the *Report* claimed that Leopold had maintained an aloof neutrality during the war free from any political involvement with the occupant. Thus instead of a positive avowal of *attentisme* the Commission simply produced a denial of the Government's accusations. The commissioners made an irreparable error when they failed to take their chance with the defense of the policy of *attentisme* and to say frankly to the Belgians: "This is what the King did for your good. He was not innocent of playing the 'waiting game,' but his concessions to innocence were made so that you might suffer less irrespective of the outcome of the war."

If, in the succeeding pages, the defense of the King's position seems weak and halting and the quotations used to illustrate and document this case often seem confused and inappropriate, all this reflects accurately the shortcomings of the defense presented by the Commission.

In the mind of many Belgians, this failure gave evidence of the very guilt that the Government was seeking to prove in its indictment. Unwittingly, the conclusions and documentation of the *Report* played into the hands of the Government.

The Prewar Period and the Eighteen-Day Campaign

The first three chapters of the *Report* discussed the behavior of the King from 1936 until 1940. This discussion was presented not only as a vindication of the King's wisdom in handling the internal and external affairs of Belgium before the war (implying that his actions during the eighteen-day campaign and during the occupation were no less wise), but it was also an attempt to silence those critics of the King who were reinterpreting past history in the light of the controversy over the royal affair. After July, 1945, many of those opposing Leopold re-examined his prewar record and claimed that the capitulation in 1940 was merely the last step in a long-planned pro-German policy. They believed that the failure to continue military co-operation with France and Great Britain and the isolated defense undertaken by Belgium from 1936 until 1940 had been deliberately designed by King Leopold to favor the Germans.

The *Report* answered these accusations regarding Leopold's role in the policy of independence-neutrality by quoting extensively from the Government's official statement published in 1941: *Belgium, the Official Account of What Happened, 1939–1940.*[5] Two quotations seemed to the authors of the *Report* to give sufficient evidence of the national enthusiasm for prewar policy.

Never did a foreign policy receive such general consent in Belgium. To be convinced of this it suffices to reread the debates of which it was the object in the Senate April 16 and 17 [1940] three weeks before the aggression. Approval continued to grow after the beginning of the con-

[5] See Chapter 2, p. 44.

flict. Even those who before had criticized it [independ-
ence-neutrality] gave it, at that time, unreserved support.
"I am even more qualified to say what I think of that
policy," said a Socialist Senator from Wallonia, "because
I was opposed to it at the beginning. Confusing independence and neutrality, I said to myself that neutrality was
. . . troublesome and cowardly. . . . But at the shock of
events which have covered human conscience in blood, I
recognized my error, and for eight months now I have
been sure that it was our young King who saw clearly.
And the old republican that I am thanks him." [6]

On September 1, 1939, the German army invaded Poland. . . . Faced with this danger, Belgium united. The
Government, in complete accordance with the King and
with the approval of Parliament and public opinion, af-
firmed the line of conduct it had been assigned since 1936.
On September 3, 1939, it published a declaration of neutrality.[7]

Regarding the defense of Belgium the Commission felt that
no better argument for the King could be made than an account of the disfavor which Nazi Germany had shown toward Belgian defense preparations after September, 1939,
preparations which had been placed under the personal
authority of the King as of September 3, 1939. The following
is a report of a meeting which took place on October 30, 1939,
between Leopold's aide-de-camp, General van Overstraeten,
and the military attaché of the German embassy in Brussels,
Lt. Colonel Pappenheim. Van Overstraeten speaks:

During the course of a recent conversation between the
German Ambassador and Mr. Spaak, it was mentioned
that the German Foreign Minister had explained the con-
centration of troops on the Lower Rhine by pointing out

[6] *Report*, p. 15.
[7] *Ibid.*, p. 17.

on the one hand, the considerable number of Franco-British troops facing Belgium, and, on the other, the Belgian redeployment directed precisely against Germany.

What I am going to tell you is neither an excuse nor an explanation. I ask you to consider it a piece of information, friendly information, which His Majesty the King thinks necessary to give to you. It is true that for a month now we have been reinforcing our units facing Germany. The reason is simple. During the first weeks of war much of our available strength was placed facing south [i.e., toward France when the Belgians feared that the French would attack Germany through Belgium]. But as soon as the Polish campaign was finished we have of necessity taken notice of the flow of the mass of the German army toward the west. . . . I wish also to call your attention to Belgian public opinion, that is to say, that of the mass of the population and not that of certain people, certain groups, or certain newspapers. If ever a German soldier should set foot on Belgian soil, the entire nation would oppose him to a man. Be convinced of this. We are an independent people, and we will not tolerate being dragged into a war, on either side, against our will.[8]

This presentation appears to be a fair and sound defense of King Leopold's role in the formulation of the policy of independence-neutrality and of the part he took in preparing the defense of Belgium. The fourth chapter of the *Report*, describing the eighteen-day campaign, gave an accurate account of the war and of Leopold's conduct in it.[9] This chapter, however, like the three preceding ones in the *Report*, was not central to the issue involved in the royal question, but served rather to create a climate of opinion favorable to Leopold. These four chapters resembled in function the speeches made

[8] *Ibid.*, p. 28. The commissioners also give evidence that it was at Leopold's insistence that the K-W line, which on September 1, 1939, was still in the planning stage, was pushed through to completion.
[9] See Chapter 3, pp. 48–55.

by Paul-Henri Spaak on July 24 and 25, 1945, i.e., to recall past events and the suspicions engendered by them.[10]

Chapter Four of the *Report* laid great stress on the ministers' constant insistence that Leopold move his armies southward in retreat toward France, a move Leopold resisted during the entire course of the campaign. The *Report* defended the King's conduct against those who claimed that he had commanded his troops in such a manner that separation from the mass of the Allied armies and surrender to the Germans would be inevitable. It emphasized that Leopold had not been an independent commander but was subject always, as his father had been during World War I, to the orders of the French Generalissimo. The *Report* documented its defense by quoting from a speech made by Hubert Pierlot at Chatham House in London on February 14, 1941, in which Pierlot admitted that any change in the disposition of Allied troops should have been made no later than May 13 or 14 and that, in any case, no adjustment could have been made in the disposition of Belgian troops without the approval of the Allied supreme commander. Such permission was never granted.[11]

The Question of Constitutionality

Chapter Five [12] was pivotal to Leopold's defense. It presented the commissioners' reasoning that the dispute over constitutionality had no place in the royal question because the issue of constitutionality had never arisen either before or at the time of the separation of King and Cabinet on May 25, 1940. The *Report* summarized the Government's case against Leopold thus:

[10] See Chapter 5, p. 109.
[11] *Report*, p. 61.
[12] Chapter Five was entitled "The Position of the King Deciding to Share the Fate of his Army."

Article 64 of the Constitution states that no act of the king can have effect if it is not countersigned by a minister. On May 25, by refusing to follow his ministers, and on May 28, by allowing himself to be made a prisoner, the King carried out a political act not only devoid of ministerial approval but also formally disavowed by his government.

Having done this, the King should voluntarily abdicate because by violating Article 64 of the Constitution, he deliberately broke the pact which united him to the nation.[13]

The defense against these charges presented in the *Report* was twofold: one, purely constitutional, which the Commission realized was insufficient to stop the controversy; the other, the heart of the defense, the denial that constitutionality was an issue.

The constitutional defense of the Commission focused on the argument that Article 64 of the Constitution did not govern the actions of the King as claimed by the Government:

> Our Commission believes that in any case Article 64 of the Constitution does not rule the matter here under discussion. While it is said that no act of the King can have effect if it is not countersigned by a minister, it only concerns, the context proves this, the act of the royal function [act of the King] and not an act of the person of the King [i.e., personal acts].
>
> Moreover, the Constitution used the word "act" on many occasions (Articles 16, 23, 56 *quater*, 69, 71, 79, 109, and 138) and each time in the same sense (act of the [royal] function).
>
> Therefore when the king decides to leave his palace or stay there, to stay in the capital or travel about the country or when he tries to avoid dangers threatening his person he does not accomplish an act in the sense of Article 64 of the Constitution and *a fortiori* he does not by so doing violate that disposition found in that article.

[13] *Report*, p. 62.

Moreover, if Article 64 declares that the action of a king, if not countersigned by a minister, is void it does not go so far as to impose on the king the obligation to follow the advice of his ministers.[14]

It is difficult to accept this peculiar constitutional interpretation which equates the decision to leave the country in order to continue a war through an exiled regime to a decision to leave the palace for an occasional journey around the kingdom. Are both actions really personal acts of the King not requiring ministerial countersignature? To answer in the affirmative would destroy any meaningful distinction between personal acts of the Monarch and actions taken in the exercise of what the Constitution calls *la fonction royale.*

Instead of trying to prove that Leopold's actions were constitutionally correct, the Commission centered its attention on an attempt to show that the question of constitutionality had never been raised either during May of 1940 or later:

But was it thus that the problem [of constitutionality] was posed to the King by the ministers? According to the documents which we have consulted it appears that the constitutional problem was not posed, theoretically and in this sense, by either the ministers or by the King during the period from May 20 to 25, 1940.[15]

The Commission contended that the Government had been concerned only with the military conduct of the war (manifested by the ministers' insistence that Leopold maintain his contact with the Allied armies and retreat southward toward France), and with the international consequences of a surrender that would indicate to the Allies that Belgium was not committed to their cause beyond the agreement to defend her own territory. To document this contention, the Commission

[14] *Ibid.,* pp. 62 and 63.
[15] *Ibid.,* p. 63.

quoted extensively from Spaak's account given at Limoges on
May 31, 1940, of the relations between the King and the Government from May 10 to May 28, 1940.[16]

> We answered that there was no hesitation possible and
> that it was the only attitude to take [concerning the King's
> question to the ministers inquiring into the wisdom of the
> departure of the Dutch Queen for England].
>   The King continued to claim that in spite of the appeal
> [for help] addressed to the French and the English he was
> without obligations toward them. We told him "Sire, you
> could have done something else had the nation permitted
> . . . but from the moment that you allowed thousands to
> be called . . . in the defense of Belgium you were bound;
> if you abandon their cause you will be a traitor and will
> be dishonored."
>   We feel that if the unhappy situation which we foresee
> [capitulation] were to be accomplished and if the min-
> isters were there to sanction it, even tacitly, by their pres-
> ence, the act which would be accomplished would no
> longer be a military act but a political one.[17]

The commissioners drew the following conclusions from the
statements made by Spaak:

> The ministers feared above all that the King would no
> longer continue the war alongside of the Allies and that
> the capitulation and the decision to remain with his sol-
> diers would be considered as a refusal to continue the bat-
> tle along with the French and the English. That attitude
> would be considered as treason and to that the ministers
> could not and would not be considered a party. . . .
>   In all the texts there is no manifestation of a single
> purely constitutional preoccupation. The only disputed
> thing is the fear of the ministers to see the King become

[16] See *Recueil*, pp. 74–95.
[17] *Report*, pp. 63–64.

involved in a situation which, on the one hand, would prevent the continuation of the battle alongside the Allies, and, on the other, would risk leading Belgium to negotiate with the occupant. There is no question of a violation of the Constitution.[18]

The Commission then quoted from both the King's account of the meeting on May 25, 1940, and from Pierlot's:

LEOPOLD: They did everything they could to convince the King . . . that by remaining in Belgium, contrary to the unanimous opinion of the Government, he would present an extremely serious question because he would be thereby responsible for the division which would occur in the country. In addition, the King would be deluding himself if he thought that he would be able to play any role whatsoever under the occupation.

PIERLOT: The Prime Minister declared that . . . the King should do everything in order to avoid capture by the enemy. . . . He could continue [if he left Belgium with the ministers] to function as Head of State alongside of the Allied governments in a political as well as in a military capacity, utilizing all the Belgian war material found in France. That is the duty of the King.[19]

It then commented on these two versions:

It was always the same preoccupation: the King should leave in order to continue the war and to fulfill the engagement contracted with the Allies. . . . Once again at that very moment [i.e., the moment of departure on May 25, 1940] when one would have perhaps expected to hear considerations of a constitutional nature regarding the possibility of the King relinquishing or not his functions other

[18] *Ibid.*, p. 64.
[19] *Ibid.*, p. 65.

than the military command, it is a simple question of fact
which the Prime Minister foresees.[20]

In short, the Commission insisted that no constitutional question was involved because no one had ever mentioned it. Only
international and military policy was involved, and the commissioners believed that the King had the same right as did the
Government to have and follow a military or international
policy, that right being contingent, of course, on the approval
that Parliament would grant or withhold after the war.

The Commission either did not wish to see or was unable to
see that the Government in May, 1940, considered unconstitutional the political actions taken by the King against the
advice of responsible ministers, though it might well be that
the Government failed to spell out this point more clearly because it seemed such a logical assumption.

The indictment of King Leopold claimed that not only the
separation of King and Cabinet but also the surrender were
unconstitutional. The commissioners took issue with the Government over the constitutionality of the King's decision to
surrender himself personally. They denied the Government's
contention that surrender was a political act and claimed instead that it was an essential aspect of the King's function as
commander-in-chief. They then reiterated their position that
ministerial countersignature was not necessary for certain
actions taken by Leopold and underlined their disagreement
with the Government over what action of the monarch required the consent of responsible ministers.

The Commission said that the constitutionality of the King's
decision to surrender had to be placed within the setting of
the last days of the campaign, particularly taking into account
the propaganda leaflets dropped by the Germans telling the

[20] *Ibid.*, pp. 65–66.

Belgian soldiers that the war was over and that their commanders had fled.[21]

It was in order to denounce the German lie, to stimulate courage, and to steel his troops for the fierce resistance demanded by the military situation that the King notified his ministers as well as his soldiers of his order of the day May 25: "Belgium expects that you do honor to the flag. . . . Whatever happens, my fate will be yours." That order of the day was unquestionably a military act from the supreme command conferred upon Leopold derived by Article 68 of the Constitution as a necessary corollary of the duty which his constitutional oath imposes upon him (Article 20) "to maintain national independence and territorial integrity." Such an act does not have to be countersigned by a minister. . . . On May 25, 1940, the King remained invested with all his prerogatives; he exercised all his functions, among them that of commander-in-chief of the army. There does not exist any pre-eminence of one function over another and even if it were otherwise, one could decide that in the midst of battle, when not only the fate of the national army but also the fate of the Allied armies were at stake, the function of commander-in-chief would have momentarily had precedence over the others by the very force of things.

However it may be, the role of commander-in-chief of the army does not consist only of assuming the direction of military operations but also of assuring success and, as a consequence, to give the orders which, by reason of the fact at his command and of which he is sole judge, are of such a nature as to achieve that end.

Thus on May 25, 1940, the King had the constitutional right to support his army using the noble language which expressed his order of the day. . . .

In reality, it is the very workings of our constitutional institutions which, by conferring various duties upon the King, have placed him, by reasons of the events which our

[21] See Chapter 3, p. 53.

constituent fathers could not have foreseen, in the position
to make a choice for which he could not be reproached
without [at the same time] refusing to recognize his constitutional power as commander-in-chief of the army.[22]

The Commission summarized its findings on the constitutionality of the surrender:

Our Commission is of the opinion that by remaining
with his army and by choosing the position of prisoner of
war, the King did not misconstrue his constitutional duties.
He adopted the solution which, according to him, the military situation demanded. . . .[23]

The remaining six chapters of the *Report* were devoted to
a defense of the position taken by King Leopold after the
capitulation and a refutation of the accusations made by Van
Acker and Spaak in July, 1945. The Commission contended that
Leopold never changed his position as announced at Berne
on June 2, 1940.[24] The *Report* quoted the following memorandum written by the King on June 1, 1940, to help document
this position:

Position of Belgium vis-à-vis England and France: until
now we have fulfilled all our engagements of neutrality
and of war. Now so long as our territory serves as a theater
for hostilities we have the duty not to allow the country to
take part in any action against those who were at its side
in the battle.
Position of Belgium vis-à-vis Germany: forced by
events, we can only accept that our territory be used for
military operations. Therefore, no possible negotiations as
long as the territory is used to aid in the hostilities.

[22] *Report,* pp. 67–68.
[23] *Ibid.,* p. 71.
[24] See Chapter 3, pp. 72–76.

Position of the Head of State: difficult because of the mentality of many Belgians and because of the position taken by the Government at Poitiers. As a consequence, the Head of State can take part in no political action as long as the country is used for military ends.[25]

It appears that although King Leopold took this position on June 2, 1940, he changed his mind before the end of the summer of 1940. It is significant that the Commission, defending Leopold's behavior and denying the accusations made against him, always harks back to this document and the evidence presented on June 2 at Berne. The *Report* fails to show later positive evidence to corroborate this position, saying that any interpretation of the behavior attributed to the King which went counter to this stance was either false or misconstrued. The *Report* presented evidence that on May 26, 1940, and on three occasions in July, 1940, various groups or persons approached the palace with suggestions that the King form a government.[26] The Commission believed that the King's refusal to act on these suggestions was proof that he intended to take no part in political action. This is not sufficient proof. First, there was no evidence that the Germans either proposed or would have tolerated such a government, or allowed any arrangement like Vichy. Second, and more important, the policy of *attentisme*, as a hedge against the future, was clearly a political action though it did not go to the extent of full identification with the enemy. (This would have made Leopold a German puppet.) *Attentisme* meant "wait and see"; a pro-German government would have meant positive commitment to the enemy, not "wait and see." But "wait and see" alone constituted political action and contravened the statement of June 2, 1940.

[25] *Report*, p. 89.
[26] *Ibid.*, pp. 98–101.

Leopold's Defense against the Government's Accusations

Frédéricq's note and the d'Ursel telegram.—The *Report* had this to say about the note from Louis Frédéricq to Le Tellier and d'Ursel:

The King was called upon at a moment (August, 1940) when the Government was dispersed to advise Mr. De Vleeschauwer who had taken the initiative which had provoked this advice. He [the King] was preoccupied lest he should deviate from the views which he knew to be those of the Government. At the same time he wished to respect the international engagements entered into by Belgium. Hence, the note of the *chef de cabinet* which, after having recalled the extent of our international agreements, contained the following counsel; not to engage military forces beyond the territory of the colony, to avoid public declarations regarding the Congo (in order to prevent reprisals), and in case of attack, to resist [the aggressor].[27]

Regarding d'Ursel's note relaying Frédéricq's information to De Vleeschauwer the *Report* said only that d'Ursel's opinions were contrary to those of the King as presented by Frédéricq and that nowhere in the Frédéricq note had the words "absolute neutrality" been used. The *Report* implied that the King's position taken on June 2 (i.e., that Belgium was still at war) remained in effect. D'Ursel's letter to the Belgian diplomatic posts throughout the world was dismissed by the commissioners as merely a compound of his original error: "We state that the two letters of the Count d'Ursel restated and developed the same theme expressed in his telegram to De Vleeschauwer,

[27] See Chapter 5, pp. 114–17.

which we have shown not to correspond to the thoughts of the King." [28]

Contrary to the defense made in the *Report*, King Leopold was exercising a political role by advising De Vleeschauwer. It must be remembered that De Vleeschauwer was the administrator-general of the Belgian Congo and Ruanda-Urundi. As far as these two territories were concerned, De Vleeschauwer exercised an absolute authority legitimately received from the Government-in-Exile. One must not forget that De Vleeschauwer had not sought Leopold's advice. Moreover, at the time of De Vleeschauwer's actions Leopold was no longer the acting executive. The Government-in-Exile had constitutionally assumed this function in May, 1940. Finally, Leopold had already said that he would not involve himself in political affairs. Considering these facts, Leopold's interference was tantamount to interference with the Government itself.

The interview at Berchtesgaden.—There were only two accounts of the interview, one written by Hitler's interpreter, Paul Schmidt, and the other written by King Leopold. The Government based its indictment on Schmidt's notes; the rebuttal made by the Commission was based on the King's account and on memorandums written by General Van Overstraeten, Leopold's aide-de-camp, before and after the meeting.

The Commission denied the Government's accusation that Leopold had solicited the audience with Hitler. It rejected Van Acker's assertion that the King "not only participated in the interview but that he was the first to bring up the political problems such as the maintenance of the Saxe-Coburg dynasty, the Belgian military regime, the control by Germany of our foreign affairs, etc." [29] The commissioners pointed out that immediately after the capitulation Hitler had sought an interview which Leopold refused. Again, it was Hitler who brought up the question of a meeting with Leopold at an in-

[28] *Report*, p. 107.
[29] *Ibid.*, p. 109.

terview between the Führer and Leopold's sister, the Princess
of Piedmont, on October 17, 1940. The *Report* also mentioned
that Colonel Goldhammer, acting in the absence of Von
Falkenhausen, the German governor of Belgium, had told Van
Overstraeten on November 1, 1940, that Germany had already lost the war because of the failure to exterminate the
British at Dunkirk. The *Report* commented:

> In passing, let us note that last phrase. That indiscretion
> committed by a high German military man could not have
> escaped the King and therefore it is perfectly ridiculous
> to suppose that by accepting Hitler's invitation, the Sover-
> eign would have aided the enemy as some have wished to
> insinuate.[30]

It appears even more ridiculous that a casual statement made
by a German colonel in November, 1940, should have caused
a total re-evaluation of Germany's future at a time when she
was at the height of her success.

To give further evidence that the audience had not been
solicited, the Commission quoted from the memorandums
written by Van Overstraeten:

> The King is preparing himself steadfastly for his dif-
> ficult duel. . . . He has conferred about it with me on
> several occasions. It is understood that his leitmotiv will
> be Belgium's material and moral distress. . . . It does not
> escape the King's observation that the Führer might pro-
> pose that he reassume the exercise of his authority. To such
> a proposal he intends to offer an absolute refusal. He does
> not conceive of exercising authority or committing any
> political act in enemy-occupied territory. He will suggest
> at the proper time the creation of a sort of Economic Di-
> rectory composed of the most illustrious men from the
> world of industry and finance, empowered to organize the

[30] *Ibid.*, p. 111.

economic life of Belgium (in reality to defend our interests against the occupant). It goes without saying that the Directory would have no political attributes.[31]

The Commission commented:

> From this text which gives the substance of the repeated conversations which the King had with his aide-de-camp one can deduce that the atmosphere at the Palace of Laeken, a week before the interview at Berchtesgaden, was neither one of defeatism nor collaboration. The King knew that the interview would be difficult, and he prepared for it with great care.[32]

The Commission wrote about the interview itself:

> In comparing the version of the King with that of Schmidt, one finds in each document a certain amount of agreement concerning those questions raised by Hitler and by the King respectively, but the Schmidt document attributes to the Sovereign a certain number of declarations of which one scarcely finds a trace in the account established by the King.[33]

The following conversation between Hitler and Leopold was taken from the notes written by the King. The reader can compare this account with that written by the interpreter Schmidt and quoted by the Government in its indictment.[34]

> Hitler asks the King if he had any personal wishes. The King responds that he has none.

[31] *Ibid.*, pp. 111–12.
[32] *Ibid.*, p. 112.
[33] *Ibid.*, p. 113.
[34] See Chapter 5, pp. 117–20. A point by point comparison cannot be made because Leopold wrote his memorandum in the first person, whereas Schmidt wrote only a third-person summary of the audience.

HITLER: I wanted to know if you have any personal views concerning the future of your country.

THE KING: I have several, but they are all subordinate to the first: I would like to have assurances regarding the re-establishment of my country's independence. Before treating the other points, I would like to be enlightened on that subject.

Hitler answered with prudence. He gave his views regarding Europe: All the countries of Europe should reach an understanding on economic grounds because the war could be long. Everyone should try to make the best of the affair.

THE KING insists: What will be the future of Belgium?

HITLER: There are two areas in which the small countries, notably Holland and Belgium, which have served as the glacis against Germany, must submit: the military and the area of foreign affairs. In internal affairs, you can do what you wish. Germany is not here to play governess for the little countries.

At the very end of the interview the King returned to the question of independence.

THE KING comes back to his original idea: May I give the assurance, when I return to Belgium, that our independence will be re-established?

HITLER: I would appreciate it if you said nothing for the moment. I would like to assure you that I will not touch your House in any event.

The King does not say anything.[35]

The Commission then concluded:

Our Commission thinks it necessary to show how the journey to Berchtesgaden remains within the limits of behavior which the King has followed from the interview

[35] *Report,* p. 114.

with his ministers at Wynendaele. The King was not ignorant of the dangers of a meeting with Hitler. Van Overstraeten's notes speak of a "dangerous duel. . . ." Nevertheless, if the Sovereign responded to the Führer's invitation at the risk of being reproached for having abandoned
his reserve as prisoner of war and of having the trip un-
favorably interpreted, he only did it for the reasons he
gave on May 25, 1940, for wanting to stay in Belgium if
he were forced to capitulate: "I am convinced that I can
serve my people better by remaining with them than by
attempting to act from abroad, notably against the rigors
of foreign occupation, the menace of forced labor or deportation and the difficulties of provisioning." These are
the terms of his letter to the King of England and before
reading it [to his ministers] he had said to them: "Beyond
the most substantial considerations from the point of view
of logic or politics there are reasons of sentiment which
one cannot bypass." We believe these words shed light on
the trip to Berchtesgaden.[36]

The matter is further complicated by the fact that the
Schmidt "report" used in Belgium after World War II was not
complete and did not represent, as Schmidt has pointed out
in his book, *Hitler's Interpreter*, the entire account Schmidt
made of the Berchtesgaden meeting.[37] Schmidt pointed out in
his book that although Leopold had solicited the interview,
probably at the instigation of his sister, Marie-José, he did not
appear to be an eager guest, nor was Hitler an eager host.
Schmidt wrote that Leopold gave every indication that he had
come to make non-personal requests of Hitler, but Schmidt
never said what these requests were. On the crucial issue of
who initiated the discussion of political issues (the Government had stated that it was Leopold who had broached the
questions), Schmidt's account in *Hitler's Interpreter* stated

[36] *Ibid.*, p. 117.
[37] Paul Schmidt, *Hitler's Interpreter* (New York: The Macmillan Company, 1951), pp. 201–5.

that, after the preliminary amenities, Hitler began one of his long monologues about the future of Europe. In the middle of it, he asked Leopold how he saw future relations between Germany and Belgium. Leopold, Schmidt wrote, replied with a counterquestion: Would Belgium recover her independence at the end of the war? Schmidt stated that Leopold came back to this question again and again, with Hitler's irritation rising at each restatement. Leopold kept insisting upon a guarantee of Belgian independence, which Hitler refused to give. Schmidt wrote that eventually Leopold and Hitler became mutually antagonistic, and the meeting was broken off much earlier than had been planned for by the Führer. The meeting had accomplished nothing either for Leopold or Hitler. Tea was served afterward because it had already been prepared, but the atmosphere was not pleasant. At tea, and this was not mentioned in the Government's indictment, it was Hitler who tried to persuade Leopold to reconsider his suggestion for closer collaboration between Germany and Belgium, but the King remained silent.

It appears that Leopold did solicit the interview and had certain questions to put to Hitler. In *Hitler's Interpreter*, however, it was not made clear whether there were any questions of political importance. After the failure to receive Hitler's guarantee of Belgian postwar independence, Schmidt wrote that Leopold withdrew into his regal dignity and refused further to negotiate. Yet after weighing all the accounts it seems that none of the evidence either in the Schmidt "report" or in *Hitler's Interpreter* is fatal to the Government's fundamental point, i.e., that it was wrong to have *any* contact with Hitler. No amount of evidence about Leopold's unwillingness to attend or his aloofness during the meeting weakens the Government's contention that to agree to such a meeting constituted treating with the enemy.

The commissioners believed that Schmidt's "report" was fraudulent. Even though a careful reading of the "report" would indicate that Schmidt was not hostile to Leopold, he did state clearly that it was Leopold and not Hitler who had solicited the interview, a contradiction of the basic fact upon which the defense made its case in regard to the meeting at Berchtesgaden. The commissioners' interpretation is inadequate. First, there is no evidence presented that would indicate what Hitler's strategy might have been. In other words, the Commission never showed what might have been the advantage to Hitler for requesting the interview. Second, in November, 1940, Hitler was the conqueror of Europe. It seems improbable that he would have had any special plan in mind for Belgium at that time other than the general design for Europe as a whole or that he would have had any particular ax to grind against Leopold personally which would have necessitated a "reinterpretation" of a past interview. Third, in the light of the postwar accusations made against Leopold, it was very much to the King's advantage to shift the responsibility for initiating the "political" part of the interview to the dead and defeated Hitler.

It appeared in the Schmidt "report," which was written in 1940, that Leopold had initiated the political discussions, while in Schmidt's book, written after the war, the initiative was shifted to Hitler. One can only conjecture at this discrepancy. In the dispute between King and Government, Schmidt's automatic sympathies would probably have been with Leopold, and the book would reflect this. Although the relationship between Hitler and Leopold had not been cordial, Leopold was never openly anti-German, and his policy of *attentisme* was adaptable to a German victory. After the war, King Leopold was one of the few major figures whose relationship with Hitler had not been totally unfriendly and who had not yet been repudiated by his people. It is not illogical to suppose that Schmidt might have tried to do what he could to help Leopold keep his throne.

The second marriage.—Perhaps the weakest part of the

Report was the attempt to prove the constitutionality of the King's second marriage. This part almost defies a clear presentation. The marriage was unconstitutional beyond doubt, but the effort to disprove this fact was so ludicrous that it only more clearly underlined its illegality. To be sure, the marriage was a tangential issue to the royal question, but the arguments used to prove its constitutionality gave strong evidence to the lengths to which the Commission would go in order to make a point. The reasoning belied the objectivity claimed by the *Report*.

The *Report* stated that when the Constitution was drawn up in 1831 the political nature of the king's marriage was recognized by those who framed the document, but the manner in which the marriage contract was to be approved and executed was not spelled out but left "under the guidance of the general principles of the constitution." [38] The Commission pointed out that "on the morrow of the proclamation of the Constitution, the question was at least implicitly resolved at the time of the marriage of King Leopold I. A responsible minister intervened and approved this act." [39]

Was this by accident? One cannot believe that the Government was able to ignore the debate which had taken place at the Congress a few months earlier [i.e., debates over the technicalities of the Sovereign's marriage], and, in any case, one fact remains, that the marriage of King Leopold I was countersigned by a responsible minister.

The marriage of His Majesty King Leopold III and Miss Liliane Baels was not like that. As a consequence, holding to constitutional principles and to the only precedent which can be invoked in the history of Belgium, one should say that, as it was celebrated, the second marriage of King Leopold III could not have any political consequences. His wife could not become Queen, and his descendants spring-

[38] *Report,* p. 140.
[39] *Ibid.*

ing from that marriage could not pretend to the constitutional rights reserved to the royal princes.[40]

Moreover, the Commission remarked:

> If the legal disposition regulating the manner in which civil and religious marriages are celebrated was not respected, the reasons must be attributed to the exceptional circumstances of the moment and of the wishes of the King and of his future wife, who understood that their marriage could not have any effect under public law.[41]

It is difficult to understand how the clear precedent of requiring ministerial countersignature for a royal marriage contract could be turned into its exact opposite simply because the King had chosen to wed a commoner and because circumstances were "exceptional."

The deportation.—Van Straelen's account of his meeting with King Leopold was the basis of the Government's accusations that the King had solicited his own deportation.[42] The Commission pointed out that on July 8, 1945, Van Straelen denied authorship of the document to Leopold's secretary, Jacques Pirenne:

> Pirenne affirmed that in the conversation which took place Van Straelen formally declared to him that the Government had no document coming from him, that he had never written such a document, that if someone claimed possession of it, it would be a forgery, and that he was ready to confirm his declaration in writing. . . .[43]

Nevertheless, on July 21, when Pirenne asked for the written statement, Van Straelen refused to sign. The Commission

[40] *Ibid.*, p. 141.
[41] *Ibid.*, p. 139. Was the *Report* saying that the best way to show the unique nature of the marriage was to show that it was not legal?
[42] See Chapter 5, pp. 121–22.
[43] *Report*, p. 145.

wrote that irrespective of the refusal, the Van Straelen document did not dovetail with the following facts:

a) On July 25, 1945, Cardinal Van Roey stated officially that many times during the occupation King Leopold had expressed the desire to be in Belgium at the time of liberation.[44]

b) Constantin Canaris, the head of the Gestapo in Belgium, testified after the war that the deportation of the King had caused confusion in Germany. Kaltenbrunner, Himmler's adjutant, had ordered Canaris on June 6, 1944, to place Leopold under guard and move him out into Germany. Canaris protested to Kaltenbrunner that Germany's most important prisoner should not be handled in such fashion. Kaltenbrunner answered that the orders had come from Hitler and Himmler and were to be obeyed without further delay. Later in Germany Leopold complained to Hitler that he was dissatisfied with his place of imprisonment and preferred a château in the mountains. Canaris testified that Hitler had asked why the King had been taken in such haste. Hitler was told that the orders had come from Himmler through Kaltenbrunner.

The Commission observed:

Of course, Canaris is a German, but it does not appear that under the circumstances he had any particular interest in denying the truth. . . . If the deportation had been solicited, at the time of Canaris' protestations to Kaltenbrunner, faced with the hesitations to execute his orders, the latter would have immediately calmed and reassured [Canaris] by telling him, if it had been true, that the deportation was desired by the King.[45]

[44] *Recueil*, p. 509.
[45] *Report*, p. 147. The statement defending Canaris' veracity was necessary in the light of the *Report's* condemnation of the veracity of another German—Schmidt.

c) On June 6, 1944, King Leopold had written General Alexander Von Falkenhausen, the German governor of Belgium, protesting his deportation.[46]

d) On the same day, June 6, 1944, Leopold wrote a proclamation to his subjects stating that he was being deported against his will.[47]

e) On June 9, 1944, the Princess de Réthy officially protested against her deportation and that of the royal children.[48]

f) Prince Baudouin (age 14) wrote to one of his friends: "I'm writing a short letter to you before leaving for captivity in Germany. It is a terrible thing, but events demand it." [49]

g) At the day of the deportation of the Princess de Réthy and of the royal children, Prince Baudouin was recuperating from scarlet fever, and his brother, Prince Albert, had the mumps.

h) At Hirchstein in Germany, the royal family was treated as prisoners in a castle guarded by armed troops and police dogs.

All these things, the commissioners remarked "scarcely harmonize with a desired and solicited deportation or one accorded as a favor by the Germans."

These versions scarcely harmonize with what a reasonable person would consider legitimate. The protestations of the King and the Princess de Réthy could easily have been a formality to rid themselves of responsibility and to court public sympathy, and the corroborative evidence of the Cardinal Archbishop is highly suspect considering that even in Belgium he is more royalist than the King. Prince Baudouin's letter is foolish evidence. Surely the Commission did not mean to sug-

[46] *Recueil*, p. 513.
[47] *Ibid.*, p. 514.
[48] *Ibid.*, p. 514.
[49] *Ibid.*, p. 515.

gest that a fourteen-year-old boy was kept *au courant* with the political machinations of his father and the palace entourage. Nor was the illness of the two princes of such a nature as to delay the execution of a long-planned event. Prince Baudouin was already on the road to recovery from scarlet fever, and the mumps could not be considered a particularly deadly disease. Moreover, a doctor accompanied the royal family to Germany.

The remaining charges.—Other significant charges made against the King by Van Acker received only passing reference, if any reference at all, in the *Report*. The telegram of condolence to the King of Italy was not discussed; the telegram to Hitler on his birthday was dismissed in these words:

> It has no importance from the moment that one knows that it was Colonel Kiewitz who alone was responsible for sending the greetings. Transmitting a humanitarian request to Berlin on behalf of the King, Kiewitz, on his own initiative, included the birthday greetings to Hitler as if they had come spontaneously from the King.[50]

The trips to Austria were not mentioned, and Leopold's entourage, to whose influence the indictment attached such great significance, concerned the commissioners almost not at all. Because the Government itself was not prepared to pass judgment on the attitudes of various members of the King's entourage, the Commission saw no reason why it should take these attitudes into consideration. If it did so, the Commission thought that it would only:

> . . . go beyond its mission, but it feels that it should reveal and underline here, the only point which should retain our attention, that in any case, the attitude of the King was always that which he had announced that it would be: total abstention from all political action. Thus, he refused

[50] *Report*, p. 118.

to receive journalists who wrote during the occupation, and he likewise avoided all contact with politicians who recommended a less retiring attitude. Far from remaining indifferent to the complacent or submissive acts of Belgians toward the enemy, he personally seized the few occasions which were given to him to give testimony to his disapproval.[51]

Summary and Conclusions

The Commission summarized its findings about the actions and attitudes of the King in this manner:

> Under all circumstances, the King appeared to have had the will to obey his conscience, a conscience inspired by the acts of his illustrious predecessors. At no time did he lose sight of the responsibilities which were incumbent on him as a result of the great position which he symbolized and of which he had the duty to assure their posterity. Moreover, we have seen him, faced with the most complex situations, trying to discern and conciliate his various duties in order to remain, at the moment of national distress, faithful to the solemn engagement which he made in the speech from the throne at the time of his accession: "I give all of myself to Belgium."[52]

In short, the Commission began and ended its *Report* from the same point of view. Leopold had done his duty under the Constitution in the light of his conscience. He was not guilty of having acted unconstitutionally but of having evaluated the situation between 1940 and 1944 in the light of different criteria from those used by the Government and Parliament. Consequently, the people of Belgium should now be given

[51] *Ibid.*, p. 134.
[52] *Ibid.*, p. 151.

a chance to decide whether they considered the course of action pursued by Leopold or that pursued by the Cabinet and Parliament as the correct one. Never did the Commission admit the proposition on which a constitutional monarchy must rest in a democratic age: that the monarch can act only on the advice of responsible ministers, and that to do otherwise would not only violate the "rules of the game" of the Belgian constitution as these had developed under Leopold's predecessors, but would also constitute an attempt to return to the predemocratic, preconstitutional forms of the eighteenth century.

CHAPTER 7

THE END OF
THE ROYAL QUESTION

The Two-Year Stalemate

THE COMMISSION's *Report* failed to gain converts to the cause of Leopold III. The four major political parties maintained their positions, and the royal question continued to await the deciding voice of the Belgian people. In the meantime, however, an armed truce was declared in Parliament. The Leopold affair was put aside so that the nation could go about other business which had been delayed too long, above all postwar reconstruction. In March, 1947, the same month in which the *Report* appeared, the tripartite Left bloc, which had governed Belgium since July, 1946, was forced to resign when the Communist ministers withdrew from the Cabinet so that their party might go into opposition.[1] The government which was formed to replace the bloc proved that for the time being the royal question was to be "ignored." The Socialists and the Catholics, the leading antagonists in the affair, governed in coalition under the premiership of Paul-Henri Spaak until the election of June, 1949.

Only two significant voices were heard during this two-

[1] The decision had nothing to do with the royal question; Communist withdrawal from the Government in Belgium was following a pattern seen throughout Europe. On May 5, 1947, they left the Government in France.

year armistice—the voice of Hubert Pierlot, the prime minister
of the exiled wartime Government, and that of Victor Larock,
a Walloon Socialist. Pierlot had hitherto taken no part in the
controversy over Leopold, but the findings and conclusions of
the *Report* prompted him to speak. He published a series of
twelve articles entitled *Pages d'histoire,* which appeared con-
secutively in the independent Brussels newspaper *Le Soir* beginning July 5, 1947. The articles were important because they
were written by one of the men most intimately involved at
the beginning of the royal question and particularly because
that man was a prominent Catholic at odds with the policy
of his party regarding King Leopold. Pierlot's articles defended his own behavior and that of his Government from
May, 1940, until September, 1944, and supported the position taken on the royal question by the parties of the Left. In
short, it was not so much the content but the source of the
articles which was significant.

With two exceptions the articles that concerned the conduct
of the war, the relationship between the King and the Cabinet
during the eighteen-day campaign, and the months of confusion during the summer and fall of 1940, added nothing that
was not already known. Indeed, they seemingly were written
with a single purpose: to recall the memory of that period and
to create a climate of opinion unfavorable to the King. They
resembled the speeches made by Paul-Henri Spaak on July 24
and 25, 1945. Nevertheless, Pierlot did make two valuable
contributions. First, he placed the royal question in its historical perspective, pointing out that the separation of King
and Cabinet on May 25, 1940, was the final episode in a long
developing controversy between Leopold and the Government
over what lay within the range of monarchical authority.
Pierlot spoke briefly of the circumstances of the prewar period
that had forced Leopold to play an active role in Belgian
affairs, a role which Leopold, abetted by Louis Wodon, had
not considered as extraordinary but as normal, provided one

accepted his conception of the role of the sovereign. Pierlot commented:

> The reinforcement of the personal role of the King in the policy of independence and soon afterward in his functions as commander-in-chief accentuated a disposition which under ordinary circumstances doubtlessly would never have had appreciable consequences because the King was not a fascist as it has been alleged and he did not think of going beyond legal means.[2]

In spite of this statement, Pierlot gave startling evidence of what Leopold considered "legal means," and this constituted Pierlot's second contribution. He helped to clarify the basic issue of the royal question, i.e., the controversy over personal monarchical prerogative under the Constitution, by showing to what dangerous lengths this personal interpretation of the prerogative could lead.

On January 10, 1940, during the "phony war," a German plane came down in Belgium, allegedly because of motor trouble. The captured pilots carried papers (which they succeeded partially in destroying) that revealed the German invasion plan of Belgium and Holland. Pierlot wrote that the Belgian government could not determine whether or not the landing was a German trick calculated to cause panic among the Belgians and to prompt their appeal for Allied aid under the 1937 agreement. Such action would have given the Germans a legitimate excuse to invade "aggressive" Belgium. The Government decided therefore to increase national watchfulness but to take no other action. King Leopold, on the other hand, on January 14, 1940, made inquiries in Great Britain:

> Without consulting a single minister, the King took it upon himself to ask of the British government, through the intermediacy of Admiral Keyes, what would be the guar-

[2] *Le Soir,* July 7, 1947, p. 1.

antees given to Belgium in case she were to call for Anglo-French assistance. The question was put by the Admiral to Chamberlain on the morning of the 14th.

The King received the answer of the British government from Keyes on the morning of the 15th. The British were prepared to enter Belgium, adding that as far as they knew, the French were ready to do the same thing. The response contained an enumeration of the guarantees.[3]

The inquiries were interpreted in London and Paris as an appeal by Belgium under the terms of the 1937 agreement, and Allied troops were massed along the Franco-Belgian border. When Daladier informed the Belgian Ambassador on January 15 that the troops were in place, the Ambassador had not the slightest idea what the French Premier was talking about. When the Ambassador questioned his Government in Brussels, the ministers were equally in the dark.

In the meantime, a meeting had been held on January 13 in the office of the chief of the Belgian general staff, General Vandenbergen. It was decided, again without the knowledge of the Government, to lower the barricades which had been placed in the roads along the southern (i.e., French) border.

> The first night (the 14th) at 1 A.M. the order was given to the southern frontier posts to allow Allied troops to enter if they were to arrive. These decisions were taken in the presence of and with the agreement of General van Overstraeten [Leopold's aide-de-camp], who was present at the conference. The Government was neither consulted nor informed.[4]

When the Government became aware of what had happened, the order was revoked, and Vandenbergen offered his resignation, which was accepted.

[3] *Le Soir*, July 9, 1947, p. 1.
[4] *Ibid.*, p. 2.

In the presence of these facts, two questions present themselves: why was General Vandenbergen designated as the author of the order sent on the night of January 13— 14? Why did Vandenbergen accept the sanctions without any reservation? I can find no other answer than this: the head of the general staff agreed to "cover" the King vis-à-vis the Government.[5]

Pierlot went on to give more evidence of the personal nature of Leopold's authority. The reader will recall that on May 25, 1940, Leopold read to his ministers the letter which he had prepared to send to the King of England.[6] Pierlot commented:

> The King came back time after time to that idea which drove him on: to obey his conscience, [to do] his duty. In his letter to the King of England . . . the King wrote: "In spite of all the contrary advice which I have received, I feel that *my duty commands me*. . . . If I felt I was able to act in that way then I would abandon the mission *which I have assigned to myself.*"
> "The mission which I have assigned to myself." Isn't that statement striking? The inspiration which the King followed was of an indisputable grandeur, but irrespective of how imperative the voice of conscience, it is not sufficient to guide those who govern. They have to keep in mind the rules of positive law, at least under a constitutional regime. Faced with a decision of the greatest seriousness, the King decided to recognize no other law than the opinion he had formed of his duty. That way of viewing the royal function differs in no way at all from personal power.[7]

The other voice heard during the two-year stalemate was that of Victor Larock, a Walloon member of the House of Representatives who wrote a series of articles for the leading

[5] *Ibid.*
[6] See Chapter 3, p. 69.
[7] *Le Soir,* July 13, 1947, p. 1.

Belgian Socialist newspaper *Le Peuple.* Fifteen articles entitled *A quand la lumière?* were published beginning September 23, 1948. The articles had only one purpose: to embarrass
the King. They were a mixed bag of fact and insinuation
based on Larock's contention that Leopold had not believed
in an Allied victory and had courted the Germans. Larock
called Leopold's policy *attentisme* and thus differs from my
opinion in only one respect: Larock believed that Leopold
thought conclusively that the Allies would be defeated. But if
Leopold was convinced that Germany would be victorious,
why play a game of "wait and see"? It seems illogical to
charge, as Larock did, that Leopold practiced *attentisme* and
also believed in an ultimate German victory:

> A treasonable policy? No, but one of supple accommo-
> dation. Not to be solidly with either belligerent; to ignore
> the resistance; to adjust to the "new order" in order to save
> the essential [things]. These were the principles of *atten-
> tisme* which the growing chances of liberation rendered
> more prudent but scarcely less pointed.[8]

Had Leopold believed in a conclusive German victory, a policy
of "wait and see" would have been unwise. It was only because he could not know for sure that he adopted *attentisme.*
Attentisme as Leopold practiced it, however, involved a
calculated risk even if the Germans should win. Leopold
would not openly collaborate with Hitler as many rulers and
crowned heads had been only too willing to do. Thus Leopold
was not completely "in favor" with Hitler, although he was not
completely "out of favor." At the meeting at Berchtesgaden
in November, 1940, Hitler had assured Leopold that his throne
would be safe after the war. The visit to Berchtesgaden only
deepened Leopold's commitment to *attentisme.* Leopold had
not been able to get Hitler to agree to a guarantee of Belgian

[8] *Le Peuple,* October 16, 1948, p. 2.

independence after the war, and Hitler had not been able to convince Leopold openly to join the Nazi cause. Thus the middle road was the only one left to Leopold. He had sought an audience which had produced nothing except perhaps the ill will of Hitler. Leopold would not openly support the Allies because in 1940 it appeared that Germany would be victorious, yet he had refused to commit himself wholeheartedly to the German cause.

The subtlety involved here is peripheral to the main issue of the royal question, i.e., whether or not the King could formulate and follow a policy not approved by responsible ministers. But since at this point (1948) Leopold still hoped to have his policy weighed favorably against that of the Government, this nuance is significant in considering the moral culpability of the King, the most vital of all considerations in the mind of the average Belgian.

Larock built his case not by speaking against Leopold but by speaking against his entourage, principally Louis Frédéricq and Count Capelle, and by denying the contention of the Commission's *Report* that Frédéricq and Capelle had maintained contact with various known collaborators in a personal capacity only without the knowledge or approval of the King.

> Can we take issue with Count Capelle for having accepted the role of intermediary? No, to the extent that he only carried out orders. Didn't *La Libre Belgique* [the pro-Leopold, conservative Catholic Brussels newspaper] write "Shouldn't a secretary be in rapport with his master?" The observation is only too true. But here is the delicate point: the collaborators whom the Count honored with his meetings saw in him the confidant of Leopold III. Received by him [Capelle] after having sought audience with the King, they were convinced that his opinions, his advice and counsel reflected the sentiments of the King. Count Capelle and the King himself could not have doubted that the interviews were interpreted in this manner. The activity of

the collaborators was powerful. They openly supported the "new order"; they served the designs of the enemy. Moreover they made no secret of their relations with the Court. They took advantage of this to preserve and to fortify their esteem with their public if they were journalists, with their subordinates if they occupied high position.[9]

On January 9, 1944, Capelle wrote to De Becker, the editor-in-chief of *Le Soir* during the occupation: "I had the honor of giving your message to the King as well as a copy of the special issue of *Le Soir* devoted to Belgian unity. His Majesty was touched by the homage and asks me to thank you." [10] Larock quoted a passage from that issue written by De Becker and praised by Capelle:

If we isolate ourselves we shall die. It no longer concerns us to choose our partners. . . . Germany and England face each other in a duel to death. . . . We have chosen. We have done so by revolutionary conviction and for love of Belgium. The destiny of our country is linked to that of the continent, its prosperity to that of Central Europe. By choosing Germany we choose Europe. Victorious Germany will expel England from the continent and will assure peace for a long time.[11]

Larock then demanded that the investigation into Capelle's activities during the occupation begun in 1946 be continued. In the summer of 1946 a preliminary inquiry was made into Capelle's association with collaborationists. The examination, conducted by a single judge without jury and attorneys, lasted for two years and ended with a *non lieu*, i.e., a declaration that there was not sufficient evidence for trial. The dossier com-

[9] *Le Peuple*, September 23, 1948, p. 1.
[10] *Le Peuple*, September 24, 1948, p. 1.
[11] *Ibid.*

piled by the presiding judge, Hussart, was handed over to
the Minister of Justice and was not made available to the
public. Larock stated that a *non lieu* was decided because, had
there been a subsequent trial, the King himself would have
been exposed. Larock wrote that the preliminary investigation
of Capelle revealed that Capelle had established contact with
Robert Poulet, editor of the pro-German newspaper *Nouveau
Journal*,[12] and that after each of the interviews with Poulet
as well as after all interviews with those involved in the collaboration, Capelle had given a written report to the King,
keeping duplicate copies for his own files.[13] Larock observed
that contrary to former statements made by Count Capelle,
those interviews were not strictly private but were known,
admitted, and controlled by King Leopold. It was revealed,
too, that shortly before the opening of the investigation into
Capelle's activities in 1946 the Count had given to the King's
secretary, Jacques Pirenne, the above-mentioned duplicates,
as well as the memorandum book in which Capelle had noted
down all appointments made during the occupation. King
Leopold had both the originals and the duplicates but refused to make them public. Larock demanded that the truth
be known claiming that the innocent had nothing to fear.
"*A quand la lumière?*"

Larock also discussed Leopold's relations with the *Légion
Wallonie*, a volunteer group of approximately 7,300 Belgians
who had fought with the Germans on the eastern front against
the Russians. Larock believed that this was an unfortunate
and pitiful group that had paid dearly for its political naïveté
by losing 3,000 men in Russia. These men were not the usual
breed of traitor; not all had been pro-German. Many were
idealists who had hoped to rid the world of communism.
Whatever their reasons for joining the *Légion*, Larock claimed

[12] See Chapter 5, pp. 112–14.
[13] There were more than twenty of these interviews, which is contrary
to an earlier statement made by Capelle that there had been only ten.

that all the men shared one characteristic—their devotion to Leopold. "The only certain fact which pleads incontestably for them is that they were never repudiated or undeceived by the King whom they believed they were serving." [14] Next, Larock dealt with Capelle's denial that he had given any form of encouragement to the *Légion*. The Count's statement had appeared in a letter to the editor of *Le Peuple* on July 11, 1945. In that letter Capelle said:

> Never did I encourage or approve (in any form, written or verbal) the activities of the *Légion Wallonie*. Never did I think, say, or write that the oath of loyalty to the King was compatible with service in the *Légion* and with the oath to the Führer. Any affirmation to the contrary is a lie. Any document declaring the contrary is false. [15]

Opposing this statement, Larock quoted an unidentified source:

> Father F. [Fierens], the chaplain of the *Légion* who honored me with his friendship and who took me into his confidence on several occasions, went back to Belgium on leave every two or three months.
>
> After having been received at the Palace of Brussels by Count Capelle, secretary of the King, he told me that the Count inquired about Commander Lippert [commandant of the *Légion*] whose brilliant qualities as an officer seemed to be known at the Palace. According to Father F., Count Capelle affirmed that His Majesty King Leopold III considered the *Légion Wallonie* a guarantee in case of a German victory, while the Belgian army at London was called to render the same service in case of an Allied victory. He held the two in equal esteem. [16]

---

[14] *Le Peuple*, October 6, 1948, p. 1.
[15] *Ibid.*
[16] *Le Peuple*, September 25, 1948, pp. 1–2.

Larock supported the above statement by the following testimony given by former members of the *Légion:*

> A letter coming from the secretariat of the King and signed by Count Capelle was communicated to the troops at the time of their stay at camp Regenwurmlager near Meseritz in August–September, 1941. According to the letter the King authorized the active officers and noncommissioned officers who had sworn an oath to him to take part in the *Légion Wallonie* if they thought that to be their duty. (Testimony of Lt. R. Wastiau, of Legionnaire A. Calui, of Lt. C. Peeters, and of Captain J. Vermeire.)
>
> During the winter of 1941–1942, a telegram came from the *Maison du Roi* to the *Légion,* which was at that moment in the Ukraine, confirming the royal approbation. (Testimony of Calui.)
>
> Father Fierens, chaplain of the *Légion* from 1942 to 1944, was in regular contact with the entourage of the King and of the Archbishop. (Testimony of Adjutant Cougnon.) [17]

Later on during the trial of Robert Poulet, Count Capelle modified his position concerning the *Légion* that he had taken in the article written to *Le Peuple* in July, 1945:

> It is true that my purposes regarding the *Légion* were varied. That is explained by the fact that I had learned that Robert Poulet had told several persons that the Palace and Count Capelle approved his actions and his articles. As a consequence I thought it my duty to be particularly circumspect regarding that which he had said. I wanted to prevent the Germans, who would have been aware of any statement made by Poulet regarding that subject, from harboring resentment against the King for having concerned himself with political questions.

[17] *Le Peuple,* October 6, 1948, p. 2.

It was because of that same reason that I never told him
[Poulet] that he was wrong to praise the intentions of certain legionnaires, but I never told him that he was right.
It was for the same reason of prudence that I told Poulet
that if Lippert, the commandant of the *Légion*, requested
an audience of the King, his request would be examined.[18]

In response to this Larock asked: "Could not this noncom-
mittal position have been legitimately interpreted by the
Légion as approval on the part of the King?"

Finally, Larock presented evidence that Leopold had taken
more than one trip to Austria during the occupation. The
following testimony was given on October 23, 1947, by L.
Rieder, a German police official whose job it had been to
accompany statesmen of occupied countries on their travels
abroad.

I was with the King of the Belgians at Heidelberg, Munich, and in Vienna where his jaw was operated on by a
dentist who lived in the area of the city hall. A Belgian
professor assisted at the operation.

After that, the King went to the home of Count Kuhn
at Nikolsburg close to the Czeckoslovakian border. He was
there four weeks, going back to Vienna from time to time
for treatment. At the end of September, 1940, he returned
to Belgium passing through Munich and Cologne.

He returned to Nikolsburg in October, 1940 [Larock
wrote in a footnote that the date was possibly an error in
transcription and should read 1941], going again to the
home of Count Kuhn. This time he was accompanied by a
woman. It was not until later that I learned that she was his
wife. He went to Heidelberg, Munich, and Vienna. After
a visit of approximately four weeks he returned to Belgium.[19]

[18] *Ibid.*
[19] *Le Peuple,* October 15, 1948, p. 2.

These articles by Pierlot and Larock did not change the basic issues of the royal question. They did, however, add weight to the moral culpability of the King, an issue of great importance during the two-year stalemate between March, 1947, and June, 1949.

Relations between King and Government, 1947–1949

Upon taking office as Prime Minister, Paul-Henri Spaak told Parliament on March 25, 1947:

> No fundamental agreement can be reached on the royal question. Each of the two parties maintains its position. Neither of the two asks the other to abandon any of its convictions. The royal question cannot be resolved at the present time, but the Government is conscious of the fact that it must promote an agreement between the parties in order to arrive at a solution which will respect our national institutions.[20]

Spaak himself broke the silence between the Government and the King in a letter to Leopold on September 25, 1947. Spaak wrote that he believed some solution could be arrived at even though the parties remained adamant in their positions. He stressed that the dispute between the Government and the King was not a moral one but one exclusively political in nature; the honor of the King, he said, was not at issue. Although this statement contradicted Socialist opinion, Spaak commented:

> It seems to me that the general turn of events permits me to say that the Socialists, while continuing strongly to criti-

---

[20] *Rapport présenté par le Secrétariat du Roi sur les événements politiques qui ont suivi la libération,* (*mai 1945–octobre 1949*), p. 110. This will be cited henceforth as *Rapport présenté par le Secrétariat du Roi.*

cize the decisions taken by the King during the war, do not intend thereby to place in doubt the motives which inspired these decisions. Thus, the difference, however important and serious it might be, that exists between the King and the Socialist party is of a purely political nature which does not have the delicate and painful character of a moral conflict. The Socialist party . . . appears to me to understand that it ought to be possible to eliminate from the discussion all [those things which] might be an affront to the person of the King as well as to the intentions which guided him.[21]

It might appear odd that Spaak, whose accusations in 1945 were aimed principally at the moral behavior of King Leopold, should now declare in 1947 that morality was no longer an issue. It is probable that Spaak had not changed his mind but only his tactics. Between 1947 and 1949 Spaak, as prime minister, was seeking a compromise. Although the constitutional issue had remained basic to the royal question, Leopold had appeared to be most sensitive to the accusations made against his moral behavior as King. Spaak probably reasoned that if the moral onus could be removed, the King might be willing to reach an agreement if he were convinced that by doing so he was not at the same time compromising his honor.

The King desired equally to have the moral onus removed, but for a different reason. In an answer to a group which had gone to Switzerland to urge him to reassume contact with the Government, Leopold wrote:

To the wish that you have expressed to see me re-exercise my constitutional prerogatives, I can have only one answer. When I swore the oath to respect the Constitution and the laws of the Belgian people, I contracted vis-à-vis the nation duties from which it does not fall to me to unburden myself. I remain ready, when it has been publicly declared

[21] *Recueil*, p. 747.

that nothing has ever stained the honor of the Head of the Dynasty, to assume responsibility.[22]

Leopold wanted to be rid of the moral stain for a reason just the opposite to that of Spaak. The King reasoned that if the stigma of his immorality could be removed from the mind of the Belgian people, they would be in favor of his return. Spaak, on the other hand, believed that if the stigma could be removed, Leopold would be willing to negotiate.

Most Belgian people cared little and understood even less about the basic constitutional issue; their primary concern seemed to be the morality or immorality of the King's behavior. Moreover, socioeconomic issues never seemed to have loomed large in the case against Leopold. From time to time, the Socialists did indicate that a return to reaction would accompany Leopold's return, but this reaction may be identified primarily with religious and ethnic issues and not with economics. An investigation into Leopold's prewar position regarding the working classes does not reveal any antilabor sentiments, and paradoxically, Leopold's association with Henri De Man, however unfortunate it may have been politically, to an extent did indicate the King's sympathy with De Man's economic philosophy, one in which the rights of labor were predominant. Furthermore, all during the royal question, the most important ally of the Socialists were the Lib-

---

[22] *Ibid.,* p. 764. Spaak made the public declaration in an address to the House of Representatives on December 10, 1947:

> As far as I am concerned I have always explained that the problem which presents itself to us does not concern the honor of the King. It concerns a political debate. . . . I want you to understand that we must do everything in our power to prevent the debate from becoming a personal quarrel which involves the honor of the Head of the Dynasty. . . . There are a certain number of Belgians who find that the King misinterpreted the articles of the Constitution. . . . There, Gentlemen, lies the debate. One can have a difference of opinion about such a point without doubting the intention and good faith [of the King]. (*Rapport présenté par le Secrétariat du Roi,* p. 117.)

erals, among whom could be found some of the wealthiest families in Belgium, anti-Catholic and anti-Leopold, but conservative economically. If, therefore, economic conservatives and economic radicals were fighting against the return of King Leopold, his economic policies must not have been a primary issue. This is well illustrated, for example, by the series of anti-Leopold articles published by the Socialist Victor Larock and by another series of similar articles attacking Leopold which appeared during May, 1949, in the Socialist newspaper, *Le Peuple*.[23] In spite of the general condemnation of the King and all his activities, socioeconomic affairs were never mentioned.

Both parties to the dispute were thus maneuvering on January 18, 1948, at the first meeting since April, 1946, between the Government and the Sovereign. The King asked Spaak: "What is the exact nature of the controversy? Is it one against me personally or is it, on the contrary, the monarchy itself which is threatened?" [24] Spaak answered that he did not consider the monarchy to be threatened, because the mass of Belgians, including the Socialists, were not republicans. At the second meeting between the Government and the King, Spaak told Leopold that it would be wise for him [Leopold] to make some statement of his position to the people since elections would be inevitable the following year as the result of new electoral laws.[25]

In a letter to the Prince Regent on June 22, 1948, Leopold expressed his opinion regarding the royal question and revived the issue of a popular consultation. The King wrote that, contrary to the position taken by Spaak on December 10, 1947, and again at the meeting on January 18, 1948, it was

[23] This series of articles was entitled *De Wynendale au Reposoir* and appeared in *Le Peuple* on successive days beginning April 23, 1949.

[24] *Rapport présenté par le Secrétariat du Roi*, p. 121.

[25] On March 27, 1948, the law was passed granting the vote to women. The electoral lists were to be revised beginning November 21, 1948, in preparation for the elections to be held in June, 1949.

impossible to attack the person of the King and not attack, at the same time, the monarchy as an institution. Furthermore, elections would not be the proper way to settle the royal affair because elections dealt with many political questions and were held within the framework of party activity. This would be quite improper, for the King was always above party:

> Today I have arrived at the conclusion that elections necessarily made within the framework of parties and dealing with the whole of political questions are not able to express the national will in a problem touching the royal prerogatives.
> It is thus that I have rallied to the idea of a consultation of all citizens authorized by law. If that consultation does not give me an indisputable majority in favor of the restoration of my constitutional prerogatives, I shall abdicate. On the other hand, if the majority is favorable to me, I expect Parliament, instructed by the national will, to use the powers given to it by the law of July 19, 1945, and put an end to the present constitutional crises.[26]

Leopold thus succeeded in destroying Spaak's strategy. Not only had the King forced the Government to state officially that the morality of the King's behavior was not an issue, but he had also told the nation that a political campaign involving the person of the King would threaten the monarchy itself. What was the reasoning behind Leopold's strategy? It seems that the strategy, largely psychological, took advantage of a nation's historic and emotional attachment to the monarchy. By having the country express itself in a consultation on the single issue of the royal question, the King would force

[26] *Recueil*, p. 799. A consultation would be a nation-wide advisory vote whose results the legislature could accept or reject. It was suggested as an alternative to a referendum whose results are binding but forbidden under the Belgian constitution. As it was conceived, however, the consultation would have differed not at all from a referendum.

out all other considerations. The people would be faced with either choosing or rejecting Leopold, yet Leopold himself had said that an attack on the King was an attack on the monarchy itself. True enough this was only the King's opinion, yet it was the opinion of one whom many of the people were conditioned by history and by emotion to respect.

On October 20, 1948, Leopold's suggestion for a consultation was rejected by the Senate. As an alternative means of deciding the royal question, the Liberals suggested that a commission be appointed to study and decide when it would be opportune for the King to resume his royal functions. A provision was made that the King send two representatives to sit with the commission. Leopold refused to consider this proposition.

> The King cannot rally to a project thus conceived. He will not agree to take part in a commission charged with saying when it would be opportune for him to resume his prerogatives. He could not take into account the highly subjective advice of such a commission.
>
> That advice could not pretend to represent that of the majority of the Belgians who would be the only ones who could lead the King to abdicate, if that opinion were unfavorable.[27]

There the matter rested. The royal question continued to hang fire until the dissolution of Parliament on May 19, 1949, prior to the elections in June.

In March, 1949, after the Government had made the decision to dissolve Parliament, contact was resumed between Leopold and the Government, and the Prince Regent also took part in the discussions. Prime Minister Spaak advised Leopold that there were only two possible positions for him to take before the elections, i.e., either to keep out of the campaign or to throw himself into it and to define his position in a

[27] *Ibid.*, p. 837.

manifesto to his subjects. Spaak suggested the first of these. At the same time Spaak also changed his approach toward Leopold. His original strategy having failed, i.e., to play down the moral issue in order that Leopold might find abdication honorable, Spaak allowed the moral issue to be re-emphasized. During the months between the Senate's rejection of a popular consultation in October, 1948, and the elections in June, 1949, the King was the subject of violent attack by the anti-Leopold press in Belgium. Leopold complained officially to the Government, saying that he remained sovereign even though in exile and was protected by Article 63 of the Constitution against personal attack. Spaak answered the complaint by recalling his address to Parliament on March 25, 1947, in which he had said that he would attempt to find some solution to the statement. He added:

> The Government feels that it has done all in its power to achieve that goal. . . . Those were our sentiments at that time. They have not changed. We regret that these rules have been violated. Violent polemics, wherever they arise, can only further poison the problems which reason and the national interest require to be resolved with dignity.
> Nevertheless, in these matters the Government can only give counsel. It has reiterated this counsel to everyone in a most pressing manner. We wish that throughout the present electoral campaign those who wish to explain themselves on the royal question do so with the moderation which the situation demands. . . .[28]

In short, Spaak would do nothing to stop the diatribes, and Leopold decided not to take an active part in the elections.

The elections, whose predominant issue was the solution of the royal question, were held on June 26, 1949, and women voted for the first time. The Minister of the Interior announced

[28] *Ibid.*, p. 848.

that the total electorate would number 2,705,182 men and 2,930,270 women, the latter being in the majority in all provinces except Limbourg. The results of the election appear in-the following table:

Table 1

The Distribution of Seats after the Elections of June, 1949
(Figures in parenthesis are the distribution of seats
after the elections of June, 1946)

Party		House	Senate
Catholic Social party	(P.S.C.)	105 (92)	92 (83)
Socialist party	(P.S.B.)	66 (69)	53 (55)
Liberal party	(P.L.B.)	29 (17)	24 (12)
Communist party	(P.C.B.)	12 (23)	6 (17)

Comparing the elections of 1949 with those of 1946, the Catholics gained 22 seats, 13 in the House and nine in the Senate; the Socialists lost five seats, three in the House and two in the Senate; the Communists lost 22 seats, 11 each in the House and the Senate. The Liberals gained 24 seats, 12 each in the House and Senate. The gains of the Liberal party had little connection with the royal question, however, but were the result primarily of a highly publicized electoral campaign championing a great reduction in the income tax. As a result of the election, the Catholic Right had 196 seats and the Left bloc had 190 seats; the Catholics won a majority in the Senate but only a plurality in the House of Representatives. The election, while reinforcing the position of the partisans of the King, revealed that the Belgians remained divided on the issue. The majority in Catholic Flanders in effect voted for the King, while the majority in Socialist Wallonia voted against him. Furthermore, the increased strength of the Catholic party in the House, 105 seats as compared to 92 in 1946, cannot be described as a gain in the popular vote, for the

Catholics increased their share of the popular vote by only 1 per cent, 43 per cent instead of 42 per cent in 1946.[29] The gain of 13 seats was due to changes in the electoral law and the redistricting of House constituencies.

The stalemate would have continued had the Liberal party not changed its position. From June until August, 1949, the three major parties attempted to form a government, but no agreement could be reached. On August 3, 1949, the Liberals issued a manifesto in which they altered their hitherto un-equivocal position for the effacement of King Leopold and supported the Catholic proposal for a national consultation. The Liberals knew that this compromise was fraught with danger: "What will become of Belgian unity on the day when the Walloons say that the Flemings imposed upon them a king they did not want, or the day when the Flemings say that the Walloons prevented the return of a king whom they wanted?" [30] Nevertheless, they considered this to be less risky than the indefinite prolongation of national crisis. They re-emphasized that their first preference was for the effacement of King Leopold and for the accession of Prince Baudouin as the fifth king of the Belgians, but they stated that if Leopold refused to agree to this, a consultation was the lesser of two evils. The party's decision to allow a consultation was based on its analysis of the results of the June elections, which showed that Liberal opinion was no longer unanimous. Whereas the Liberals in Wallonia and Brussels remained over-whelmingly opposed to King Leopold, Liberal opinion in Flanders had become more fluid. The party added, however, that if its proposal were to be accepted the results of the consultation would have to be more than a simple majority:

It is necessary that in each region of the country at least half the people pronounce in his [the King's] favor; it is

[29] *Les élections législatives du 4 juin 1950* (Institut De Solvay, Bruxelles: Editions de la Librairie Encyclopédique, 1953).
[30] *Recueil*, p. 857.

necessary, too, that he receive [the vote of] at least two-thirds of the whole electorate.[31]

The Liberals suggested that Leopold make his opinion known regarding their proposal.

The King answered in a message dated August 5 that he would have to be guided by the Constitution:

> I have been asked if I would consent to fix a specific percentage which I would consider necessary in order to reassume the exercise of my prerogatives. My answer to that question can only be dictated by the Constitution. . . . It has been suggested, by evoking the two-third's rule which is demanded for every constitutional change, that the same percentage be applied to the consultation. That proposal is not justified since the Constitution and the law provide that Parliament by a simple majority name the Regent, state the end of the "impossibility to reign," and determine when the throne is vacant.
>
> In order to be constitutional the consultation can only be considered as an opinion rendered by the electorate to Parliament and to the King.
>
> By the law of July 19, 1945, Parliament reserved for it-self the power to decide the end of the "impossibility to reign." It therefore falls to Parliament, clarified by the national consultation, to pronounce the end of the "impossibility to reign," in full liberty and under its own responsibility.
>
> It would be inadmissible . . . for the King thus to restrain the powers of Parliament.[32]

These words can only be called smug, the words of a man to whom a compromise was offered but who rejected it as beneath his dignity, taking refuge behind constitutional niceties. Leopold could not have failed to realize that a consultation, no matter how camouflaged, was unconstitutional. He

[31] *Ibid.,* p. 858.
[32] *Ibid.,* p. 861.

himself had suggested a consultation several times before, and the pro-Leopold party had been the first to place the proposal before Parliament in 1945. Then and subsequently it was rejected as unconstitutional. In 1949 it was no less unconstitutional, but the Liberals, eager to put an end to the dangerous schism that had existed in Belgium for almost ten years, were willing to make concessions. Leopold did not deny the constitutionality of a consultation because he reckoned that such a consultation could be *favorable* to him. He denied the constitutionality of a fixed percentage larger than a simple majority because these results could be *unfavorable* to him. Leopold held out for a consultation whose results would be determined by a simple majority, yet even these results he would not consider absolutely binding:

> I do not intend to be tied to specific figures. When I declared in my letter of June 22, 1948, that I would abdicate "if this consultation does not result in an indisputable majority in favor of the restoration of my constitutional prerogatives" I wanted to make known that in considering the results of an eventual consultation, my only care would be to conform *to what appeared to me,* without any possible doubt, to be the will of the nation, taking into account not only the number of votes cast but also the circumstances which accompanied the consultation and the inferences drawn from these circumstances.[33]

On August 11, 1949, the Catholics and the Liberals formed a coalition cabinet under the premiership of the Catholic Gaston Eyskens. They agreed to hold a consultation, but no details were announced. The Socialists expressed their firm opposition thus:

> Does the Parliament need further clarification by means of such a consultation? The P.S.B. does not think so. The

[33] *Ibid.,* p. 862. Emphasis added.

balloting of June 26 was sufficiently significant . . . following which the P.S.C., having placed at the head of its program, as in 1946, a solution identical to that set out in the King's message, received only 2,187,310 votes, whereas 2,604,421 male and female electors decided in favor of the parties opposed to that solution.[34]

Furthermore, the Socialists declared that if, in spite of their opposition, a national consultation were held, they would consider a simple majority insufficient and a personal interpretation of the results by the King as totally inadmissible:

> It would be inexcusable to expose the country to the dangers of a popular consultation if it did not bring about a definite solution to the royal question. A discussion would inevitably spring out of the problem of interpreting the results if no accord were reached beforehand regarding the subject.[35]

The Consultation

The Eyskens Government spent the fall months of 1949 preparing for the consultation. A legislative commission was appointed by the Government to study the constitutionality of the consultation. The Commission's report appeared on December 22, 1949, and supported the consultation. The report included a minority note written by Victor Larock, the author of *A quand la lumière?*, and a fellow Socialist from Flanders, Henri Fayat, disagreeing with the majority opinion and declaring the consultation to be unconstitutional.

The report and the minority note were of interest, but not so much because of their findings and opinions—these were predictable considering the political composition of the Com-

[34] *Ibid.*, pp. 862–63.
[35] *Ibid.*, p. 864.

mission. It was the reasoning behind each opinion which was remarkable. The majority opinion, basically Catholic, claimed that the consultation would be an advisory vote and not a referendum, and it pointed out that the Constitution was silent on advisory consultations. The majority reasoned that the legislature had residuary powers to handle those things not specifically forbidden by the Constitution. Had not the legislature interpreted the Constitution and used its residuary power when it passed the law of July 19, 1945, regarding the Regency? The Constitution was silent regarding the manner in which the Regency should be brought to an end, and the legislature was legitimately entitled to interpret this silence:

> The Houses dispose of the residue of sovereignty. Beyond their legislative or political function they exercise the sovereign function in the place of the nation from which all power is derived. The fundamental principle of our constitutional law flows from the existence in Belgium of a parliamentary constitutional regime as well as from Articles 25 and 78 of the Constitution.[36]

The minority note, on the other hand, interpreted the consultation in the opposite light.

> Such procedure [the consultation] was not provided for by any disposition of the Belgian constitution and one would take great liberty with regard to the latter to pretend that, on such an important point which touches so intimately the functioning of our representative regime, omission was the equivalent of permission. . . . To justify . . . the constitutionality of the project by evoking the residuary sovereignty of the legislative power, to support [the contention] that the Houses are able to adopt such a

---

[36] *Rapport fait au nom de la commission spéciale sur la consultation populaire au sujet de la question royale* (Chambre des Représentants, 22 décembre 1949; Projet de loi instituant une consultation populaire au sujet de la question royale), p. 13.

project for the simple reason that nothing in the Constitution explicitly forbids them to do so is, in reality, to pretend that the Houses can reverse constitutional order indirectly when they are not able to do so directly.[37]

Whether or not the two major parties realized it, they were reversing their basic position on the royal question. Hitherto, the Catholics, by defending King Leopold and his ideas about the monarchy, had been supporting a conservative, legalistic interpretation of the Constitution, claiming that the Constitution was to be interpreted and enforced strictly to the letter as it appeared in the document of 1831 and in its subsequent amendments. The Socialists, on the other hand, by opposing King Leopold and his theories of the monarchy, had been supporting, under the impact of universal suffrage and political parties, a broadened interpretation of the Constitution and its amendments. According to them power had come to rest in a strong legislature which could interpret the Constitution in the light of evolving customs, whether or not such customs had been formally added to the basic law. The law of July 19, 1945, gave to Parliament the authority to determine when the Regency should come to an end. At that time, the Socialists and their allies argued that because the Constitution was silent on the matter, Parliament could legislate and thereby fill in the gap left in the Constitution. In 1945 the Catholics had rejected this line of reasoning, claiming that Parliament could not act merely because the Constitution was silent. Now in 1950 the reasoning was reversed. Catholics championed a broadened interpretation of the powers of Parliament under the Constitution, while the Socialists clung to a narrow legalistic conception.

On March 12, 1950, approximately 5,500,000 Belgians (the total number voting in the elections of June, 1949, was 5,-635,452) went to the polls to answer this rather ambiguous

[37] *Ibid.*, pp. 38–40.

Table 2

Consultation of March, 1950, Results by Province in
Actual Number of Ballots Cast and in Percentage

Province		Ballots Cast	
		Actual Number	Per-centage
Flanders			
Antwerp	Yes	514,889	68
	No	241,011	32
East Flanders	Yes	529,789	71.8
	No	207,737	28.2
West Flanders	Yes	430,778	74.7
	No	146,040	23.3
Limbourg	Yes	——— ᵃ	83
	No	——— ᵃ	17
Wallonia			
Liége	Yes	244,678	41.7
	No	341,182	58.3
Namur	Yes	115,373	53
	No	102,551	47
Hainaut	Yes	267,311	35.8
	No	477,207	64.2
Luxembourg	Yes	83,696	67
	No	44,445	33
Brabant (Brussels area including Brussels)			
	Yes	554,173	50.6
	No	530,405	49.4

ᵃ Correct figures not available.

question: "Etes-vous d'avis que le Roi Leopold III reprenne l'exercice de ses pouvoirs constitutionnels?"[38] It was agreed

[38] The question posed to the electorate was ambiguous for the very reasons that Victor Larock had pointed out in his minority note: "An affirmative response is perfectly clear. A negative response is obscure. 'No' could signify either abdication or the postponement of the question. . . . Many in good faith believe that they have to choose between a return to the throne and the indefinite suspension of power." (*Rapport fait au nom de la commission*, pp. 50–51.)
Many, too, were of the opinion that a vote against the King was a vote for a republic. The Catholics did little to quash this erroneous belief.

Table 3

"Yes" Vote in Consultation of March, 1950; P.S.C. Vote in
1949; Liberal Vote in 1949; Combined P.S.C. and Liberal
Vote in 1949, by Provinces, in Percentages

Province	P.S.C. Vote 1949	Liberal Vote 1949	Combined Liberal and P.S.C. Vote 1949	"Yes" Vote 1950
Limbourg	73	10	83	83
East Flanders	52	15	67	72
West Flanders	56	13	69	75
Antwerp	51	11	62	68
Luxembourg	58	16	74	65
Namur	43	12	55	53
Brabant	37	22	59	50
Liége	32	15	47	41
Hainaut	25	14	39	36

that the ballots would be counted on a regional basis, i.e.,
Wallonia, Flanders, and Brussels, but no percentage was
officially decided upon. On October 18, 1949, a joint communiqué had been issued by Leopold and Eyskens in which
Leopold declared that if the percentage in his favor was less
than 55 per cent he would not reassume the exercise of his
prerogatives. He did not say, however, that he would abdicate.[39]

Balloting was secret and compulsory, but each elector had
the option to cast a blank or deliberately invalidated ballot;
2,933,392 electors (or 57.68 per cent of the *valid* ballots) voted
"yes," while 2,151,881 (or 42.32 per cent of the *valid* ballots)
voted "no." Approximately 10 per cent of the *total* ballots cast
were *invalid*. Table 2 gives the results of the consultation in
actual ballots cast and in percentage by province. Table 3
compares by province the vote on the consultation with the

[39] *Recueil*, p. 872.

ballots cast in 1949 by the Catholic party and by the Liberal party, the two parties supporting the consultation.

The country as a whole voted for Leopold by 57.68 per cent, but in Flanders the pro-Leopold vote was 72 per cent. All the Flemish provinces voted for his return. Wallonia voted against Leopold by 58 per cent, and Brussels voted against him by 52 per cent. Yet, in Wallonia, only two provinces voted against him by more than 50 per cent, Liége by 59 per cent and Hainaut by 64 per cent. Both these provinces were areas of heavy industry and mining and were the largest centers of Socialist strength in Belgium. In Flanders the province with the lowest percentage favorable to the King (68 per cent) was Antwerp, the port of whose major city, Antwerp, was a stronghold of the Federation of Socialist and Communist trade unions (F.G.T.B.). The province with the highest percentage favorable to the King (83 per cent) was Limbourg in Flanders, predominantly agricultural and considered to be the most conservative and Catholic in the nation. Brabant offered the most interesting phenomenon. This is the province in which Brussels is located and is the only province bisected by the language frontier, i.e., the invisible line which separates Flanders from Wallonia. In other words, Brabant is approximately half French-speaking and half Flemish-speaking. It split 50–50 on the consultation, while the city of Brussels voted against the King by 52 per cent.

Comparing the "yes" vote in 1950 with the election results in 1949, one observes that in Flanders the percentage favorable to the King in 1950 was larger than the combined vote for the Catholic and the Liberal parties in 1949, while in Wallonia the percentage was smaller. In Flanders, the consultation verified what the 1949 election had indicated, the strong pro-Leopold sentiment among Flemish Liberals. The increase in the consultation over the combined Catholic-Liberal vote in 1949 can be attributed in part to votes from the minor Flemish parties that had drawn ballots away from the Catholic party in 1949 but which remained pro-Leopold on the royal question, and in part to other defection from the Left. According to a study made by the Solvay Institute of the University of Brussels, in the country as a whole, about 15 per cent of the members of parties on the Left voted against their party's position on the royal question. This was true particularly of the Liberal party, and if the reader compares Wallonia with Flanders, this was particularly true in Flanders. In Wallonia and in Brussels the consultation seemed to indicate that party regulars in both the Catholic party and the Liberal party abandoned their party to show their opposition to Leopold.

The Liberals, who had been responsible for the compromise which had allowed the consultation, now refused to vote with the Catholics to implement the law of July 19, 1945. They considered the percentage favorable to Leopold to be too small to satisfy their requirements.[40] Although the Liberal party would not vote for Leopold's return, it agreed to continue negotiations with him. The Catholics and the Socialists, on the other hand, remained adamant, the Catholics for an unconditional resumption of power, the Socialists for abdication. Parliament was once again at an impasse.

On March 14, 1950, Prime Minister Eyskens left Brussels for Geneva to receive Leopold's decision. The King refused to act and threw the initiative back to Parliament:

> The national will has been clearly expressed. Under the circumstances, I can only remain at the disposition of the nation. True enough, the fact that the royal question has become an element in the platforms of political parties is not without difficulty. But these exclusively political difficulties are not my responsibility. I personally only assume the obligations which are derived from my dynastic role.
>
> It is up to Parliament to take political responsibility. In virtue of the power conferred upon it by the law of July 19,

[40] See this Chapter, pp. 182–83.

1945, the organs of national sovereignty must without further delay solve the present crisis.[41]

Leopold's maneuverings were beginning to darken the mood of the nation; above all, the Flemish-Walloon animosity was growing ominous. On March 19 the National Walloon Congress (a Walloon separatist organization) met at Namur:

> The permanent committee of the National Walloon Congress states that the national consultation has underlined the division of Belgium into two totally opposed groups; it states that the great majority of the citizens of Wallonia and Brussels has pronounced clearly against the return of Leopold III; it considers that the resumption by him of his royal prerogatives would seriously disturb the duty of Walloon loyalty to the Belgian state; it calls all organizations hostile to the return of the King to unite in common battle; it salutes with great emotion the thousands of workers who have been engaged in the battle until now; it affirms its irrevocable will to bring about by all the means in its power the triumph of the cause of Wallonia, part of the cause of democracy and liberty; it decides to sit permanently and to keep ready for any eventuality.[42]

On the same day, another separatist group, Free Wallonia, spoke of breaking away from Belgium if the King should return:

> The general council of Free Wallonia . . . proclaims that the restoration of Leopold III would have as its consequences the disaffection of the Walloons with regard to the Belgian state and [proclaims] that the Walloon movement could be led to revise its doctrines and demand the liberation of Wallonia in conformity with the charter of the United Nations.[43]

[41] *La Libre Belgique,* March 17, 1950, p. 1.
[42] Taeda, "De la consultation populaire au message royal," *Le Flambeau,* XXXIII, No. II (April, 1950), 169.
[43] *Ibid.*

The religious issue, too, became a serious part of the growing conflict:

> Moreover the maneuverings after the consultation have crudely displayed the desire of the Flemish clergy to establish their hegemony over the whole of Belgium. They plan, under the cover of a King who has become their instrument, the planting on our soil of a regime [like that of] Salazar. . . .[44]
>
> The clergy, at the instigation of its chief [Cardinal Archbishop Van Roey at Malines] has waged an open campaign in favor of the return of the King. Cardinal Van Roey has gone so far as to invoke in his [the King's] behalf the fourth commandment (Honor thy Father and thy Mother), and Monsigneur de Tournai publicly censured Chanoine Demine, who had the temerity to think . . . that the royal question was a free question.[45]

On March 19, 1950, Eyskens and his coalition Catholic-Liberal cabinet resigned, unable to solve the dilemma. For the next two weeks, first Eyskens, a Catholic, and then Albert Devèze, a Liberal, tried in vain to form a new government. On March 19 the Socialists, at an extraordinary national congress declared by the unanimous vote of 1,162 delegates:

> The P.S.B. remains disposed to try any peaceful national solution other than the return of Leopold III to the throne. . . . The action committee will continue and will extend its activity by all the means in its power until Leopold III, finally understanding that the interest of the country passes beyond his [personal interest], makes room for the fifth King of the Belgians.[46]

On March 22, Paul-Henri Spaak appealed to the King to consider the greater good of his country and to abdicate in favor

[44] *Ibid.*, p. 179.
[45] *Ibid.*, p. 166.
[46] *Ibid.*, p. 168.

of his son. Spaak said that the Sovereign should consider that his honor had been vindicated by the results of the consultation and should step down:

> Sire, the discussion which swirls around your person is fundamental and essential: it is the very functioning of our institutions; above all, it is the approval or condemnation of that which we thought we should have done during the war, at the hour of battle, for our independence and for our liberty. It is the whole concept of the Fatherland, of its interest and its duty. When all that is at stake, the minority will not give way; it will continue the battle. . . . Sire, Belgium, its unity and prosperity are in danger. Everything that the majority wants is not necessarily good; everything that is legal is not necessarily to be recommended.
>
> The great statesmen are those who first prevent certain problems from arising, and then who know how not to abuse victory.[47]

Spaak's appeal went unheeded. As a result, both Eyskens and Devèze failed to form a government, and on April 6 Prince Charles charged the Catholic Paul Van Zeeland with the task. The Liberals announced that they were still willing to compromise and would support Leopold's return but not unconditionally. The Catholics stood their ground, and Van Zeeland rejected the Liberal compromise. At this point the Liberals withdrew all support from Van Zeeland and rejoined the Left in its opposition to King Leopold. It was once again clearly the Catholic Right against the combined Liberal, Socialist, and Communist Left.

On April 13 Van Zeeland, still attempting to form a cabinet, flew to Geneva to consult with the King. On April 17 Leopold issued a statement which, for a moment, offered a measure of hope. For the first time he expressed the willingness to com-

[47] *Le Peuple,* March 22, 1950, p. 1.

promise. He would temporarily delegate power to his son, retaining for himself, however, the right to declare when that delegation had come to an end. In Belgium the statement was considered ambiguous. The Left saw the delegation as an indirect means whereby Leopold could reascend the throne. At a round table discussion of the King's proposal, the three major parties again reached a stalemate over attempts to agree on answers to the following questions: (1) Should the declaration of the end of the Regency and the delegation of power to Prince Baudouin take place simultaneously (in other words, should Leopold be allowed to reassume his powers even for a limited time)? (2) How long would Leopold remain in Belgium (in other words, would Leopold appear for the formal delegation of authority to his son and then resume his exile)? (3) Under what conditions would the King consider that it was time to reclaim for himself the powers of Head of State?

Leopold refused to help in resolving the stalemate. On April 24 he expressed pique at the parties for suspecting his intentions:

> In taking the initiative to attempt to put an end to the present crisis . . . you know full well that I was guided only by the desire to assure a just equilibrium between the rights of the majority and those of the minority and to make possible a reconciliation between Belgians.
>
> I will not hesitate to say that I am astonished . . . to witness the discussion that has come up regarding my presence in the country. . . . Guided by the proposals which had been submitted to me I made a suggestion; let it be accepted in the spirit in which I presented it. . . . There is no need whatsoever for guarantees which can add nothing to the value of my word.[48]

It appeared that the immovable object had met the irresistible force. As a result, on April 30, 1950, the Prince Regent dis-

[48] *La Libre Belgique*, April 26, 1950, p. 1.

solved Parliament and called for elections to be held on June 4.

The Elections of June 4, 1950, and the End of the Leopold Affair

As a result of the elections the Catholics received an absolute majority of seats in Parliament, though they did not receive an absolute majority of votes in the country, as shown in Tables 4 and 5. The increase in Catholic strength in the elections of June, 1950, as compared to the elections of June,

Table 4

Actual Vote and Percentage of Total Vote Cast for the House of Representatives by Each of the Parties in the Elections of June, 1950, Compared to the Figures for the Election of June, 1949

Party	1950		1949	
	Votes	Percentage	Votes	Percentage
P.S.C.	2,354,965	47.69	2,190,898	43.55
P.S.B.	1,704,360	34.51	1,529,720	29.75
P.L.B.	557,019	11.28	767,180	15.25
P.C.B.	234,325	4.75	376,765	7.49

Table 5

Distribution of Seats in the House of Representatives after the Elections of June, 1950, Compared to the Distribution after the Elections of June, 1949

Party	1950	1949	Gain or Loss
P.S.C.	108	105	+3
P.S.B.	77	66	+11
P.L.B.	20	29	−9
P.C.B.	7	12	−5

1949, was due in part to the fact that the P.S.C. had been able
to prevent the formation of small, right-wing Flemish parties
and in part to pro-Leopold members of parties of the Left,
primarily the Liberals, who had to vote P.S.C. if they wanted
to support the King. The Liberals lost in part because they
were not able to carry out their fiscal program while they
were in the Government from August, 1949, until March,
1950, and in part because of their vacillating position on the
royal question. Many Liberals who wanted to be sure that
opposition to Leopold would not slacken voted for the Socialist
party even though by June, 1950, the Liberal party was once
again firmly in opposition to the King. The success of the
Socialist party was due primarily to the reasons given above
but also to the appeal that it made for middle-class votes, a
new phenomenon in Socialist campaigning.

The distribution of party strength in the various provinces,
shown in Table 6, indicates that the parties maintained their

Table 6

Percentage of Total Votes Secured by the Various Parties in
Each Province in the Election of June, 1950

Province	P.S.C.	P.S.B.	P.L.B.	P.C.B.
Flanders				
Antwerp	51	40	7	2
East Flanders	58	27	12	3
West Flanders	62	26	11	1
Limbourg	78	20 [a]		2
Wallonia				
Liége	33	46	13	8
Namur	45	42	10	3
Hainaut	26	52	12	10
Luxembourg	62	35 [a]		3
Brabant (Brussels area)				
	41	38	16	5

[a] Joint Liberal-Socialist ticket.

traditional strongholds. Limbourg again voted overwhelmingly for the Catholic party, but in Antwerp, industrial and dock workers reduced the Catholic strength in Flanders. Brussels again divided almost evenly between Socialists and Catholics, with the Liberals holding the balance. In Wallonia, the Socialists maintained their strength as the Catholics had in Flanders, but Luxembourg, the southernmost province of Wallonia, continued to give a strong majority to the Catholic party, for Luxembourg is essentially rural and deeply conservative.

On June 8, 1950, a Catholic cabinet was formed under the premiership of Jean Duvieusart. That same day, the Socialists in the House of Representatives threatened the Catholics:

> The Socialist group in the House states that the P.S.C. owes to the Flemish vote (the champions of *incivisme*) the gain of three seats which it has obtained in the House. It denounces before the country the extremely grave character of the decision announced today according to which the first action of the Government will be to call a joint session of the two Houses in order to bring the Regency to an end and to recall Leopold III to the throne.
>
> The Socialist group believes that by acting in this manner the P.S.C., which did not receive 50 per cent of the votes in the country as a whole, is deliberately rejecting the solution which alone can lead to national agreement; that it [the P.S.C.] abuses intolerably a majority of four seats; that it scorns the clear significance of the only election which the Constitution recognizes, i.e., that of universal suffrage, which offers startling proof that Leopold III is only the king of an essentially regional and partisan majority; and that the P.S.C. is placing the personal causes of the King above the evident and immediate interests of the working class and of the middle classes which have so long been neglected.
>
> The Socialist group addresses a solemn warning to the

P.S.C. that it will never accept that our form of government be placed before a *fait accompli* by a majority acquired at the price of justice and of a shameful alliance.

Knowing that our democratic institutions as well as our civil and social peace are in peril, the Socialist group will wage merciless war in Parliament, and if Leopold III is called back because of the wishes of his partisans, the Group and the Party will not cease to oppose both the King and his party.[49]

On June 27 Duvieusart announced that Leopold would soon return. That same day, the F.G.T.B. declared that if Leopold returned, the members of the Federation would no longer recognize him as king. On July 6, 1950, the Catholic government called the Houses into joint session for the purpose of implementing the law of July 19, 1945. The session began amidst violent opposition within Parliament itself, and within Wallonia, in Brussels, and in the larger cities of Flanders. The debate which raged for the following two weeks added nothing that was not already known about the royal question. It is enough to say that the debate was a violent résumé of ten years of conflict. Considering the composition of the Houses, the vote at its conclusion on July 20 was inevitable.

By July, 1950, however, what was happening in Parliament was no longer important. Political action had failed, and the anti-Leopold forces were beginning to take direct measures of reprisal. On July 6, the first demonstrations began against the return of Leopold. In Charleroi workers struck for half an hour; in Liége, forty mines went on strike and workers' demonstrations took place in Le Centre. On July 9, 80,000 workers came to Brussels to pay homage to the Prince Regent and hear Paul-Henri Spaak praise the Regent, while everyone knew he was condemning the King:

They thank you for never having despaired of the fate of the Fatherland, even during the blackest days of the

[49] *Le Peuple*, June 9, 1950, p. 1.

war; for having shown your complete fidelity to our Allies, aiding them by having taken part in the Belgian resistance; for having carefully avoided all contact with the occupant and for having preferred the dangers of going into hiding to deportation.

They thank you for having accepted, on the morrow of the liberation, the difficult task of Regent, for having exercised your functions in a scrupulously constitutional manner, for having done everything to maintain the prestige of the country, for having been the symbol of the unity of your compatriots.[50]

That the speech was illogical, that it was impossible to compare the wartime behavior of the captive Sovereign to that of his brother who held no position of authority until September, 1944, was no longer important either to the speaker or to the audience. There was only one objective, to prevent the return of Leopold, and every device, legal or illegal, would be used to accomplish it.

On July 10 there were demonstrations in Antwerp against the King, and between July 10 and 12 the entire "black country," the coal mining area centering on Charleroi, was paralyzed by strike. On July 12, 20,000 workers marched through Charleroi carrying banners with inscriptions such as: "Leopold III, symbol of unity of the *incivique* Catholic Party"; "Leopold III, the repudiated King without respect either at home or abroad"; "We defy Leopold III to put foot in Charleroi." On that same day there were strikes in Ghent, Namur, Mons, Le Centre, and in the Borinage. On July 14, the anniversary of the fall of the Bastille, 10,000 demonstrators poured into La Louvière screaming "Leopold to the gallows"; "Abdication"; "Down with Leopold!"; "Hang him, hang him!" The demonstrators listened to Max Buset, the president of the Socialist party:

[50] *Le Peuple,* July 10, 1950, p. 1.

We find ourselves now in the Chambers [of Parliament] sitting in joint session with the "yes-men" of Malines. ["Les 'ja-ja' de Malines." "Ja" is Flemish for yes; Malines is the seat of the Cardinal Archbishop.] There will be no *joyeuse entrée* for their Beloved. I defy the Government to announce the day and the hour of the *joyeuse entrée*. There will be no speech from the throne. Leopold will not speak. When he shall ask for consultations not one Socialist will respond to his appeal. The Socialist ministers of state will resign. You will see! We will give back our decorations with an expression of our contempt. The P.S.B. solemnly declares that it repudiates the King; that it no longer recognizes him as king of the Belgians. The P.S.B. declares solemnly that it will carry the fight until abdication! [51]

That same day, July 14, there were strikes and demonstrations by the F.G.T.B. at Verviers. Some of the banners carried by the pickets read: "Sire, your son is our King"; "Our Queen Astrid did not deserve this"; "Would you accept Liliane Baels as Queen?"; "Shh, don't speak of the resistance! Leopold is listening!" The President of the Regional Committees of Communal Action of the F.G.T.B. told the demonstrators:

He is the king of one party, the P.S.C., which because of its majority wishes to reinstall a Saxe-Coburg-Gotha despite the working class which will not stop the fight until the king of the Germans has abdicated. During two wars, our soldiers fought for liberty against foreign tyranny. They do not want the workers to accept today a dictatorship which would be installed on the throne along with Leopold III. [52]

The Catholics remained deaf to the opposition, and on July 20 the united chambers voted to end the Regency. A total of 197 Catholics and one Liberal voted for the King; the So-

[51] *Le Peuple*, July 15, 1950, p. 1.
[52] *Ibid.*

cialists, the Communists, and the remaining Liberals left the chamber and refused to vote. On July 22, King Leopold, Prince Baudouin, and Prince Albert returned to Belgium. They arrived early in the morning and were driven immediately to Laeken.[53] During the afternoon the King addressed his subjects by radio and asked them to unite and forget, but half the population was willing to do neither. The next day there were mass meetings at Liége and Brussels. Paul-Henri Spaak told the crowd gathered at the Place des Martyrs in the capital:

> We are in a relatively difficult situation. "Relatively" because our adversaries are completely wrong if they imagine that they have won this battle which has lasted since May 25, 1940. The King refused to follow the advice of his ministers in order to be able to continue that foreign policy which he had premeditated, that monstrous policy which placed on the same footing the Germans who had attacked us and the Allies to whom we called for help.
>
> This fight has gone on for ten years. This is not the final phase. We Socialists have decided to continue the combat. Perhaps we will lose this or that battle, but because we represent political honor and the memory of resistance, and because our cause is fine and just, we will eventually win! [54]

On July 26 the Regional Committees of the F.G.T.B. met at Charleroi to hear Arthur Gailly tell the delegates:

> The object of our battle is the abdication of Leopold III. The King is responsible. . . . We have only one resource to make him listen to reason. He will have to hear our complaints because this time we will act. The future depends on him and on him alone; one word, only one word, and the movements which we are about to unleash

---

[53] Even in 1960 Belgians speak of the "cowardly" return in the early morning hours when there would be few people on the streets.

[54] *Le Peuple*, July 25, 1950, p. 1.

will stop immediately; if not . . . the strike. . . . It will be total, resolute, firm, disciplined.[55]

On July 27 thousands of demonstrators marched through the streets of Brussels singing *La Marseillaise* and *L'Internationale* and chanting "Leopold to the gallows!" "Abdication!" One-half block from the doors of Parliament, at the corner of Rue Royale and Rue de la Loi, Spaak joined the agitators and led them to the royal palace. There pro-Leopold demonstrators met anti-Leopold groups and shouts of "Long Live Leopold" "Down with Leopold" "To Moscow" "*Incivique*" mingled with each other. That same day the F.G.T.B. sent a letter to Prime Minister Duvieusart announcing the first strikes which would gradually spread and paralyze the entire national economy. The next day, July 28, there were approximately 500,000 strikers in Wallonia. The trains leaving Belgium were held up at the frontier, and highways were impassable after strikers had covered them with nails. By July 30 the strikes were almost total throughout Wallonia, and in Flanders, the port of Antwerp could no longer operate. Barricades were built in the streets of Liége, and at Grâce Berleur, near Liége, three Socialist demonstrators were killed by the police. In the capital, insurgent strikers controlled half the railroad stations, and transportation within the city was at a standstill. Violence broke out between the tramway workers belonging to the non-striking Catholic union and those of the striking Socialist union. From France trade unionists came across the border illegally to aid their Belgian brothers, and by July 31, 100,000 demonstrators had started to march on Brussels. The roadblocks which were set up on and around the plains of Waterloo were ineffective, and the demonstrators infiltrated by the thousands into the capital. Belgium was poised on the edge of civil war.

On July 30 the National Confederation of Political Prisoners

[55] *Le Peuple*, July 26, 1950, p. 1.

and their Descendants (no more unbiased and apolitical group could be found in Belgium) called a meeting to which were invited the leaders of the three major political parties. All agreed, including the delegates from the P.S.C., that abdication was the only solution if Belgium were not to be torn apart by revolution. A delegation was sent to Leopold and was received by him at 1 A.M. July 31. At 2 A.M. a cabinet meeting was called which lasted until 7:30 A.M. The remainder of the day was spent in conferences between the Government and the leaders of the three major political parties and finally between the Government and the King, his secretary and his personal secretariat. At 8 P.M., July 31, Leopold agreed to abdicate, but the communication announcing his decision was delayed until the following morning. During the night Leopold had misgivings. He had agreed earlier to delegate power to Prince Baudouin, who would ascend the throne as king automatically on September 7, 1951, on his twenty-first birthday. Leopold sought one last time to reserve for himself the right to decide, in consultation with his ministers, when the delegation of power to Baudouin should come to an end. His attempt failed, and at 6:45 A.M., August 1, 1950, the Minister of Public Education read the message of abdication to the press. On August 3 the abdication was submitted to Parliament, and on August 11, 1950, Prince Baudouin, now Prince Royal, took the oath of office as prescribed by Article 80 of the Constitution.

CHAPTER 8

SUMMARY
AND CONCLUSIONS

THE ROYAL QUESTION left bitterness not only among the Belgian people but also in the young Prince who had become a king in spite of himself. Among the people, the alienation was not simply between the Flemings on the one hand and the Walloons and citizens of Brussels on the other. In the capital and in each of the provinces there were Catholics, Socialists, and Liberals on both sides of the question, and divisions could be found even within families. The Belgians say that the royal question was to Belgium what the Dreyfus case was to France, and they tell of fathers who refused to speak to sons, and brothers who became estranged because of their attitudes toward Leopold.

The Prince, in 1950 a twenty-year-old man who had known only imprisonment and exile since he was ten, felt hatred toward those Belgians who had repudiated his father and who had turned so venomously against the Princess Liliane whom he loved as his mother. The years of confinement and exile had drawn the royal family closer together than possibly it would have been under normal circumstances, and the Prince considered himself the usurper of the place deserved by his father. As a result, few changes were made at Laeken following the abdication. Ex-King Leopold, his wife, and their family remained in the palace, and the young King continued to live in the quarters which had been his when he was a child. Leopold's entourage became Baudouin's entourage, and for all practical purposes, Leopold remained King. During the first years of his reign, Baudouin never allowed the people to forget this.

There was political estrangement, too, between King Baudouin and the leaders of the major political parties, but strangely enough, Baudouin vented his anger not against the Socialists and the Liberals who had led the opposition against his father, but against the Catholics who Baudouin felt had forsaken the ex-King. The relationship was friendly between Baudouin and the Socialist Achille Van Acker, who became prime minister in 1954 and headed the Government until 1958. On the other hand, Baudouin completely ignored the Catholics and refused to receive in audience some members of the P.S.C. Nevertheless, when the Catholic Gaston Eyskens again became prime minister in 1958, a *détente* was reached, and the Catholics tried to re-establish harmony between the party and the Sovereign. It is probably because of this that the Catholics allowed Baudouin considerable independence of action, and the King took full advantage of this generosity. It must be quickly pointed out, however, that it was not mere generosity on the part of the Government, because the latitude allowed Baudouin extended only to problems of the Congo, an area where the kings have traditionally played a much more significant role than in either domestic or international affairs.[1]

On three occasions after 1958 Baudouin was active in Congolese affairs. Following the uprisings in Leopoldville on January 4, 1959, it was the King and not the Cabinet who told the country in a radio address on January 13 that it would

[1] Before the Congo became a Belgian colony on November 15, 1908, it had been the personal possession of King Leopold II. He almost forced his huge fief on the nation, which at that time considered the area, ninety times larger than Belgium, to be a costly and troublesome burden. The nation left this "unwanted child" partly in the care of the Belgian kings. Even when the colony began to reveal its enormous wealth this tradition was maintained.

soon have to consider independence for the colony. Only a few of the ministers knew what the King would say in his speech, and although these few were sufficient to take responsibility, it is significant that it was Baudouin who first spoke of independence.[2] Afterward, it was Baudouin who successfully opposed the removal of Governor-General Cornélis, whose policies many of the ministers no longer favored. Finally, the King surprised the Government (again, only a few knew of his plans) by flying to the Congo in January, 1960, at a time when most of the ministers feared for the King's safety should he travel in the colony, and were concerned politically lest his presence lead to demands which might worsen the already sensitive relations between the Congo and the mother country. The opposition notwithstanding, Baudouin insisted that he was insufficiently informed by his entourage and wanted to see for himself.

By the end of the 1950's the Belgians began to realize that Baudouin was becoming a king in his own right. After almost ten years, it appeared that he was beginning to enjoy his role as sovereign and to appreciate the importance of it. In the relationship between Sovereign and subjects, the turning point was Baudouin's trip to the United States in May, 1959. The King showed to the Americans a side of his personality that the Belgians had never seen before. Baudouin laughed in public for the first time; he received the press for the first time; for the first time he talked to the "man in the street" and moved among many levels of society. He danced, went to parties, and met movie stars. He had what appeared to be a tremendously good time, while at the same time he impressed the American people with his dignity and wisdom. The American senators and representatives will probably long remember Baudouin's sobering observation made in a speech to a

[2] This was an unfortunate situation when one realizes that after the bloodletting which followed the independence of the Congo on June 30, 1960, there were many Belgians who blamed King Baudouin for his premature words.

joint session of Congress. In his appeal for world peace, he commented that it took twenty years to make a man but only twenty seconds to destroy him.

The Belgians were happy about Baudouin's reception in the United States, but they also were a bit dismayed. Had their King displayed a personality reserved only for strangers? Perhaps, as the Belgians came to realize, the strangers had been warmer to Baudouin than his people had been, and he in turn had responded to that warmth. Not to be outdone, the Belgians gave the King a frantic welcome home. Hundreds of thousands lined the streets of Brussels to see him and to cover him with shouts of praise and bouquets of flowers. It appeared at last that the bitterness left by the royal question was beginning to pass, and to add to the good feeling, Leopold announced that he, the Princess Liliane, and their children were moving from Laeken to a château on the other side of Brussels.

Armed with the growing good will of his people and the sense of authority that his part in the Congo affair had given him, would Baudouin forget the lesson of the royal affair? There is evidence that the King would not or could not. An incident regarding the King's brother Albert showed to what degree the King's will was still able to withstand public pressure. In April, 1959, Albert became engaged to the Italian Princess Paola Ruffo di Calabria, and Pope John XXIII agreed to marry them. Without consulting his ministers the King announced that the marriage would take place at St. Peter's in the Vatican. The Belgians were disappointed. There had been no royal spectacle since the marriage of Leopold III to Princess Astrid in 1926, and there had been no gaiety at Laeken since her death in 1935. Now, the people were to be deprived of this wedding. The Socialists took up the opposition and gave it a constitutional basis. Belgian law requires that the civil marriage ceremony precede the religious, but since there was no civil law in the Vatican, the marriage would be imperfect under Belgian law. The Vatican answered that Vatican City was also a state and that consequently the marriage would carry civil sanction, but the Socialists were not convinced and refused to reconsider. At this point, June, 1959, the Vatican resolved what threatened to become another impasse between clericals and anticlericals by withdrawing its invitation. King Baudouin argued no further and announced that the ceremony would be performed in Brussels. (This was a minor issue but one which clearly demonstrated the nature of the relationship between sovereign and government.)

The royal question confirmed once and for all the principle that the king reigns but does not rule. Except in those areas in which the king is granted or allowed a degree of independent action, he has only three rights: the right to be consulted, the right to encourage, and the right to warn. If, in the execution of these rights, he is opposed by his government, he must give way to it. Regarding the Belgian king's right personally to command his troops in battle, a commission appointed by the Ministry of Justice reported in July, 1949, that this would never happen again because of the nature of modern warfare; future wars would be waged by experts not by executives. Only in dealing with the Congo did the king retain after 1950 discretion which could lead to conflict, but as this study is being completed in the summer of 1960, the Congo has already become an independent nation. Consequently there is now no area of traditional discretion open to the Belgian king, and he reigns today under the Constitution as interpreted in the light of the outcome of the royal question. It is significant that the Constitution remains exactly as it was before the royal affair. There have been no amendments to codify any particular alteration in the power of the king. The change has come about by means of a political process which sanctioned the evolved custom. With the Constitution unchanged, the area in which the King *could* use his authority remains as broad as ever, but because nothing has been specifically limited, everything has been tacitly circumscribed. This result was not deliberately planned, but this is the situation as it now exists.

In the first chapter of this study, it was stated that a strong king was needed to unify the Belgian people, yet today the power of the king has been greatly weakened. Does this mean that national unity will suffer as a result? Such a development seems unlikely. Fortunately, the internal factors which have contributed to disunity have lost strength in the past few years. In 1958 the major political parties agreed on a *pacte scolaire* which settled for the next twelve years the dispute over the problem of state aid to Catholic schools.[3] The bitterness over the royal question becomes milder as the years pass and Baudouin gains the deeper affection of his people. Moreover, international affairs are contributing to a sense of national unity. *Incivisme* appears less important today when the former great antagonists, France and Germany, seek a rapprochement. The Belgian people will be forced to rally all their strength as they seek to adjust to the loss of the Congo. They can no longer afford to let petty internal division sap the energy which must be centered elsewhere, particularly on economic survival. Finally, Belgium's role in the vanguard of the "new Europe," her hope that the economic organizations of which she is now an enthusiastic member (e.g., the European Coal and Steel Community, Euratom, and the European Economic Community) will lead to a political federation of western Europe, is forcing upon her a reappraisal of her own disunity. Belgians cannot expect to live comfortably with their neighbors if they cannot live comfortably with each other.

Will the monarchy become unnecessary as the Belgians draw closer together? Closeness does not eliminate difference; it only alters the mentality in which that difference is accepted. Belgium remains divided into two proud groups, neither of

[3] Signed on November 6, 1958, and ratified by the House of Representatives on May 6, 1959.

which by itself is Belgium. The phenomenon of national unity manifests itself solely in the person of the king. With national unity the king becomes the symbol of mutual pride that draws the Walloons and the Flemings together and ceases to be the symbol and the referee of the antagonisms which have historically pulled them apart.

If we accept Ernest Barker's definition that democracy is not a solution but a means of seeking a solution, a means of nonviolent choice between alternatives, then the ultimate resolution of the royal question was not in the spirit of democracy.[4] The end was democratic because it removed power from the hands of one and distributed it more equally into the hands of several, yet the means used were not democratic if we are willing to agree that revolution, including civil war, is not the ultimate alternative in the game of democratic politics. If, however, one of the parties in the game of democratic politics, even if that party represents the majority, is so unwilling to compromise and flouts the rules which protect the minority, does not that minority have the right to resist, and if pushed to the limit, to rebel? An affirmative answer may be given if the minority fears that its existence as a minority is threatened by the action of the majority, or if the "rules of the game" itself are being altered by the majority without the consent of the minority.

At the time when the royal question came to a head, the minority—composed of Socialists, Liberals, and Communists, but represented primarily by the Socialists—feared that both these possibilities would become actualities. The consultation of January, 1950, had shown that the anti-Leopold bloc was in the minority, but only by a small percentage, and the elections of June, 1950, were won by the Catholic pro-Leopold forces by a popular vote of only 47 per cent, yet a percentage which gave them an absolute majority in Parliament. Thus the Left

[4] Ernest Barker, *Principles of Social and Political Theory* (Oxford: At the Clarendon Press, 1951), p. 207.

anti-Leopold bloc feared that if the Catholics, who were primarily Flemish, carried the day in regard to the royal question it would set a precedent whereby a mere majority could always govern. With Flanders containing the majority of Belgians, the Walloons feared for their political life.

At the same time a solution of the royal question favorable to Leopold would have changed the "rules of the game" of the Belgian monarchy as it had come gradually to be modified since 1831 under the influence of universal suffrage and responsible political parties. While a pro-Leopold solution of the royal question would not have involved any direct modification of the Constitution, Leopold's return would have declared that under the Constitution a king could espouse and follow a policy which had been rejected by responsible ministers. If Parliament could not decide between king and cabinet the final voice would always be that of Parliament and ultimately that of the people. Nevertheless, the workings of a modern constitutional monarchy would have been seriously threatened irrespective of who had the final voice. The Socialists, who had for years been seeking to reduce the king to a figurehead, could not have tolerated such a solution, and the Catholics acted in complete disregard for historical change and commonly accepted "rules of the game" by insisting on such a solution.

Why had the major antagonists reached such an impasse by midsummer of 1950? The answer to this question, the reader should recall, has been suggested in Chapter 1. A modern constitutional monarch is the embodiment of historical continuity and national self-identification, but he functions successfully in this capacity only if there already exists a tradition common to each of his subjects and if the people, of which he is the reflection, are whole and able to be mirrored in a single, undistorted image. *The monarch, in other words, is the result, not the cause of homogeneity and consensus.* The question of consensus is at the center of the royal question. For the average Belgian, the affair focused all the other issues over which there was lack of harmony in Belgian society—the ethnic, linguistic, religious, and economic problems discussed in earlier chapters.

Those who drew up the Constitution in 1831 knew that because of disparate and antagonistic elements within Belgian society, political agreement would be almost impossible over certain sensitive issues, and no accommodation in Parliament based exclusively on a free acceptance of the "rules of the game" would be sufficient to counterbalance this lack of concordance within the society itself. As a substitute for the lack of consensus in both society and Parliament, the king of the Belgians was given considerable power under the Constitution. He thus occupied a unique position; he represented the societal unity which would be nonexistent without him, and he was granted sufficient power to maintain and propel the unity he embodied.

The reader saw in earlier chapters that as new groups began to enter political life, they demanded an increasingly larger share of power. This increase was made possible in part by decreasing the power of the king. At the same time, however, a weakened king would have to be counterbalanced by a stronger legislature. A strong legislature under the parliamentary system demands that the "rules of the game"—the procedural rules of Parliament, particularly the basic rules of discussion and compromise—be firmly entrenched and fully respected. But if compromise within Parliament is to be tolerated and respected, the elements of division within society cannot be too deep. In speaking of what we would call today consensus among the British, Lord Balfour once remarked that the British people were so fundamentally at one that they could safely afford to bicker. This was not true of the Belgians in the years which preceded the royal question. The historic elements of disunity were maintained, and, if we consider the friction between Walloons and Flemings between

1920 and 1940, those elements were strengthened. In short, no change could come about which would result in greater agreement in Parliament until the elements of consensus within society were strengthened.

Given the above considerations, there could be no solution short of revolution if ever the conflicting elements in Belgian society were unwilling to compromise on a particular issue. This is what happened in the royal affair. Civil war did not break out only because one party gave way before the threat of force by another. Yet what did the royal affair prove regarding national consensus if unity was the result of coercion? It demonstrated that force, though it cannot compel consensus, can shock a nation into the realization that the only alternative to agreement on fundamental issues is a breakdown in that society's governing machinery. This is the same alternative which presented itself to the second Austrian Republic after World War II. In 1934, because of lack of consensus among the ruling elements in Austrian society, the republic was dissolved and replaced by a dictatorship. Learning a lesson from the destruction of Austrian democracy in 1933–1934 the historic enemies, the Socialists and the Christian-Social Conservatives, have ruled in coalition since 1945. They have done so not because they trust each other but simply because the one will not trust the other to rule alone. Nevertheless, the shock of what happened in 1933–1934 has at least produced a going political concern.[5]

Three sets of circumstances seem to point to a solution of the problem of consensus in the Belgian polity and society. There is, first of all, the realization of how close the country had come to civil war and disintegration. Next, there is the evidence on the part of the numerical minority of 1950 of how far it is prepared to let the other camp proceed with the modification of certain "rules of the game." Finally, there are

[5] See Alfred Diamant, "The Group Basis of Austrian Politics," *Journal of Central European Affairs,* XVIII, No. 11 (July, 1945).

forces at work which tend both to unify Belgium internally and to integrate her into a wider European community. The continued industrialization of Belgium and the general modernization of many western European societies contribute to the continued lessening of the traditional ethnic, religious, and linguistic cleavages. This has been happening in France as well as in Belgium. Furthermore, Belgium's enthusiastic participation in common European institutions has forced the people, as was pointed out above, to bury their internal differences and bend their efforts to the common European enterprise.

But even without the help of any of these forces and events, the royal question, by forcing Belgians to consider the costs of disunity, has caused them to clarify the limits of agreement and disagreement and has thereby strengthened the cohesion of Belgian society and stabilized the political process.

EPILOGUE

BELGIUM HAS SUFFERED recurrences of strife since this study was completed in the summer of 1960. The most serious broke out over the proposal made by the Catholic-Liberal government, and opposed by the Socialists, to enact austerity legislation designed to mitigate the loss of the Congo and to adjust Belgium to the new economic order in Europe. This occurrence calls for no modification of my earlier appraisals, however. The way in which the crisis was met in fact suggests that the Belgians will probably resort increasingly to a device similar to that used by the Austrians: the Catholics and Socialists, the antagonists, will govern in coalition whenever serious problems demand solution.[1]

The austerity program, *la loi unique*, presented on November 7, 1960, called for increased taxation and reduced welfare benefits. Walloon opposition was fierce. The hostility was led by the Socialist party and by the F.G.T.B., and resistance was particularly intense to the provisions which would tighten social security aid. Wallonia has been hard hit in recent years, especially in coal-mining and related industries, and unemployment is a serious problem. Curtailment in welfare payments would fall heaviest in Wallonia.

The Socialist party challenged the Catholic-Liberal program, and the F.G.T.B. called for massive strikes to demonstrate its opposition. The walkouts began on December 20, 1960, and were almost complete throughout Wallonia. There was a lull over Christmas, but the intensity increased immediately afterward, and the strikes soon spread to Brussels and

[1] See Chapter 8, p. 214.

216

to the rest of Belgium. Rioting, which caused several deaths, reached such frightening proportion that the Government had to call Belgian NATO troops from Germany to help keep order.

After Parliament reconvened in January, 1961, following the holiday adjournment, the Socialists sought in vain to have *la loi unique* withdrawn, but the Government was resolute. To this point, there is much reminiscent of the July days of 1950. But the Socialists became alarmed at the growing violence of the strikes and they announced a willingness to compromise. The party would reluctantly accept *la loi unique* provided that those articles dealing with social security be submitted to the tripartite Commission for Labor and Employment. The Government accepted the bargain. The House passed the law on January 13, and the Senate voted its approval on February 13. In the meantime, the strikes had come to an end, and Belgium was peaceful again.

On February 17, however, the victorious governmental coalition fell apart over differences between the Catholics and the Liberals on an electoral reform law and on the methods for applying *la loi unique.* On February 20, Parliament was dissolved after King Baudouin imposed two stipulations: (1) the Catholic-Liberal coalition would remain in office until the elections, and (2) *la loi unique* would not be put into effect until after the new Parliament had assembled.

In the elections held on March 26, the Catholics won 96 seats in the House; the Socialists, 84; the Liberals, 20; the Communists, 5; and the Flemish Nationalists (*Volksunie*), 5. In the Senate the Catholics were elected to 47 seats; the Socialists to 45; the Liberals to 11; the Communists to 1; and the Flemish Nationalists to 2. A Catholic-Socialist coalition government was formed with Théo Lefèvre (P.S.C.) as prime minister, and Paul-Henri Spaak (P.S.B.) as vice-premier.[2] In

[2] Spaak had recently returned to Belgian political life after his resignation as secretary-general of NATO.

his policy statement to the House, Lefèvre announced that the controversial provisions of *la loi unique* would be re-examined. On May 5, the new government received a vote of confidence from the House; six days later the Senate gave its approval.

What does the solution to this crisis indicate in the light of the solution to the royal question? It appears that neither the Catholics nor the Socialists can pass legislation unwanted by the other irrespective of the majority either might command alone or in coalition with a third party. Moreover, the Catholics and the Socialists in coalition seem to give to one another a sense of responsibility that each party appears to lack by itself. Belgian political stability rests on the marriage of convenience of its two major parties.

The potential productiveness of the marriage became evident in Feburary, 1962, when the Government established a permanent linguistic frontier. It hoped to accomplish a reduction in the chronic tension which exists between Walloons and Flemings. The linguistic border between Wallonia and Flanders, with Brussels as a bilingual enclave, was made stationary; no longer would it vary after each ten-year census. The problems in making the new law work will be extraordinary, but the arrangement represents a step in the direction of concord and demonstrates the good that can result when the two major parties work in harmony.

BIBLIOGRAPHY

In addition to printed material found in Belgian libraries this study is documented with information gathered during formal and informal conversations. The author was in Belgium from September, 1958, until December, 1959.

PRIMARY SOURCES

Government Documents and Semiofficial Publications

Almanach Royal (officiel). Publié depuis 1840 en exécution de l'arrêté royal du 14 octobre 1839. Bruxelles: Imprimerie E. Guyot, 1935–1950.

Annales parlementaires de Belgique: Chambre des représentants et sénat, 1945–1950. Bruxelles: Imprimerie du *Moniteur Belge*, 1945–1950.

Annuaire administratif et judicaire de Belgique et de la capitale du royaume. Bruxelles: Etablissements Emile Bruylant, S.A., 1935–1950.

Belgique, La relation officielle des événements, 1939–1940. Publiée par le Ministère des Affaires étrangères de Belgique. London: Evans Bros., Ltd., 1941.

Contribution à l'étude de la question royale. 2 vols. Edité par le groupement national belge en collaboration avec la centrale belge de documentation. Bruxelles: S. A. Edimco. 1946.

Documents on German Foreign Policy, 1918–1945. 10 vols. Washington, D.C.: U.S. Government Printing Office, 1949–1957.

Guide des ministères. Revue de l'administration belge, secrétariat. Bruxelles.

Rapport de la commission chargée d'émettre un avis motivé sur l'application des principes constitutionnels relatifs à l'exercice des prérogatives du roi et aux rapports des grands pouvoirs constitutionnels entre eux. Ministère de la Justice. Bruxelles: Imprimerie du *Moniteur Belge*, 1949.

Rapport de la Commission d'Information instituée par S. M. le roi Léopold III le 14 juillet 1946 et note complémentaire. Luxembourg: Imprimerie St. Paul, 1947.

Rapport fait au nom de la commission spéciale sur la consultation populaire au sujet de la question royale. Chambre des représentants, 22 décembre 1949; Projet de loi instituant une consultation populaire au sujet de la question royale.

Rapport présenté par le Secrétariat du Roi sur les événements politiques qui ont suivi la libération (mai, 1945–octobre, 1949). Bruxelles: Imprimerie et Publicité du Marais, 1949.

Recueil de Documents et Supplément. 2 vols. Etabli par le Secrétariat du Roi concernant la période 1936–1950. Ixelles: Imprimerie et Publicité du Marais, n.d.

Books and Memoirs of Participants

CAPELLE, COMTE DE. *Au service du roi.* 2 vols. Bruxelles: Charles Dessart, 1949.

DE MAN, HENRI. *Cavalier seul, 45 années de socialisme européen.* Genève: Editions du Cheval Ailé, 1948.

SCHMIDT, PAUL. *Hitler's Interpreter.* New York: The Macmillan Co., 1951.

SECONDARY SOURCES

Books and Pamphlets

L'attitude de Léopold III de 1936 à la libération. Paris: Editions Albin Michel, 1949.

Jane's Fighting Ships. London: S. Low, Marston and Company, Ltd. Vol. 44.

Le roi et son peuple. Anvers: Editions Le Papegay, 1945.

ALEXANDRAKIS, M. D. *De l'exercice du droit de dissolution par le pouvoir exécutif. Etude critique et de législation comparée.* Paris: A. Pedone, 1937.

AMERY, L. S., RT. HON. *Thoughts on the Constitution.* London: Oxford University Press, 1947.

ANSON, WILLIAM R. *The Law and Custom of the Constitution.* Oxford: At the Clarendon Press, 1892.

ARNESON, BEN A. *The Democratic Monarchies of Scandinavia.* New York: D. Van Nostrand Co., Inc., 1939.

BAGEHOT, WALTER. *The English Constitution.* New York: D. Appleton and Co., 1884.

BARKER, SIR ERNEST. *Essays on Government.* Oxford: At the Clarendon Press, 1951.

———. *Principles of Social and Political Theory.* Oxford: At the Clarendon Press, 1951.

CAMBRELIN, GEORGES. *Le drame belge, 1940–1950.* Paris: Paul Mourousy, 1951.

CAMMAERTS, EMILE. *The Prisoner at Laeken, Fact and Legend.* London: The Cresset Press, 1941.

CAMPION, LORD, AND LIDDERDALE, D. W. S. *European Parliamentary Procedure: A Comparative Handbook.* London: George Allen and Unwin, Ltd., 1953.

CHARLES, EDMOND. *Le second mariage du roi devant la constitution.* Namur: *La Nouvelle Gazette,* 1948.

———. *La question royale et la constitution.* Mons: Union des Imprimeries, 1947.

CHLEPNER, B. S. *Cent ans d'histoire sociale en Belgique.* Bruxelles: Université Libre de Bruxelles, Institut Sociologie Solvay, 1958.

CHURCHILL, SIR WINSTON. *Their Finest Hour.* Boston: Houghton Mifflin Co., 1949.

CORNIL, GENERAL HRE. FERNAND. *Détresse et espérance.* Bruxelles: Editions Ferd. Wellens-Pay, 1944.

DABIN, JEAN. *Le problème constitutionnel de la reddition du roi.* 1948.

DE CORTE, MARCEL. *Mon pays, où vas-tu?* Bruxelles: Editions Universitaires, 1951.

DE LICHTERVELDE, LOUIS, LE COMTE. *Léopold II.* Bruxelles: Editions Universitaires, Les Presses de Belgique, 1926.

———. *Léopold Ier.* Bruxelles: Librairie Albert Dewit, 1929.

———. *Essai sur notre monarchie nationale.* Bruxelles: Goemaere, Imprimeur du Roi, 1919.

———. *La structure de l'état belge.* Louvain: Collection d'études de doctrine politique catholique. Editions Rex, n.d.

———. *Le pouvoir royal.* Bruxelles: Groupement d'études politiques, Cahier No. 1, n.d.

———. *La monarchie belge.* Paris et Bruxelles: Librairie Nationale d'Art et d'Histoire, G. van Oest et Cie., Editeurs, 1921.

———. *Métier de roi: Léopold I, Léopold II, Albert I, Léopold III.* Bruxelles: Editions Universitaires, Les Presses de Belgique, 1945.

DE LIEDEKERKE, RAOUL. *Examinons l'affaire du roi.* Bruxelles: chez l'auteur, n.d.

DELSINNE, LEON. *Le Parti Ouvrier Belge.* Bruxelles: La Renaissance du Livre, 1955.

DENDIAS, MICHEL. *Le renforcement des pouvoirs du chef de l'état dans la démocratie parlementaire.* Paris: Editions de Boccard, 1932.

DE PAEUW, LEON. *Albert, troisième roi des Belges.* Bruxelles: Anc. Etabliss. J. Lebègue et Cie., S.A., 1934.

DE PANGE, JEAN. *Le roi très chrétien.* Paris: Librairie Arthème Fayard, 1949.

———. *Comment se fait un roi.* Paris: Plon, 1937.

DUMONT, GEORGES-H. *La dynastie belge.* Bruxelles: Editions et Ateliers d'Art graphique ELSEVIER, 1959.

———. *Léopold III, roi des Belges.* Bruxelles: Charles Dessart, 1944.

FABRE-LUCE, ALFRED. *Une tragédie royale: L'affaire Léopold III.* Paris: Flammarion, 1948.

FINER, HERMAN. *The Theory and Practice of Modern Government.* New York: Henry Holt & Co., The Dial Press, 1949.

FIRKET, MAURICE. *Un mauvais coup-manqué.* Liége: Editions de la *Nouvelle Revue Wallonne,* n.d.

GANSHOF VAN DER MEERSCH, W. J. *Le commandement de l'armée et la responsabilité ministerielle en droit constitutionnel belge.* Bruxelles: *Revue de l'Université de Bruxelles,* 1949.

———. *Des rapports entre le chef de l'état et le gouvernement en droit constitutionnel belge.* Bruxelles: Editions Emile Bruylant, 1950.

GERARD, JO. *Tempête sur le palais.* Bruxelles: Pierre Blanc, 1952.

GIRAUD, EMILE. *Le pouvoir exécutif dans les démocraties d'Europe et d'Amérique.* Paris: Recueil Sirey, 1938.

———. *La crise de la démocratie et le renforcement du pouvoir exécutif.* Paris: Recueil Sirey, 1938.

GOFFIN, ROBERT. *Le roi des Belges, a-t-il trahi?* New York: Editions de la Maison française, 1940.

HAAG, HENRI. *Rien ne vaut l'honneur—l'église belge de 1940 à 1945.* Bruxelles: Editions Universitaires, Les Presses de Belgique, 1946.

HAEGELSTEEN, PIERRE. *Le parlement et le statut royal.* Anvers: La Métropole, 1953.

HÖJER, CARL-HENRIK. *Le régime parlementaire belge de 1918 à*

1940. Stockholm, Uppsala Och: Almqvist & Wiksells Boktryckeri, AB, 1946.

HOOVER, HERBERT. *Hoover Book, The Belgian Campaign and the Surrender of the Belgian Army.* New York: Belgian-American Educational Foundation, Inc., 1940.

HOUDRET, CHARLES. *Le roi impossible.* Paris: Les Editions de la Nouvelle France, 1949.

INSTITUT DE SOLVAY. *Les élections législatives du 4 juin 1950.* Bruxelles: Editions de la Librairie Encyclopédique, 1953.

JENNINGS, W. IVOR. *Cabinet Government.* Cambridge: At the University Press, 1947.

KAMMERER, ALBERT. *La vérité sur l'armistice.* Paris: Editions Médicis, 1944.

LAHAYE, HILAIRE. *Complot vu par un historien de l'an 2,200.* Ypres: Hilaire Lahaye, 1950.

L'HOIST, ANDRÉ. *La guerre 1940 et le rôle de l'armée belge.* Bruxelles: Editions IGNIS, 1940.

LARMINIER, ROBERT. *Les paladins du roi.* Veltem: Robert Larminier, 1952.

LAROCK, VICTOR. *Un aspect de la question royale: A quand la lumière?* Bruxelles: Société d'Editions du *Peuple*, 1948.

MATIVA, A. *Le roi.* Bruxelles: Librairie de Lannoy, 1924.

MEIRE, R. J. *Ecrits et discours de sa majesté le roi Léopold III.* Anvers: Editions Sheed and Ward; Bruxelles: Editions Erasme, n.d.

MONTGOMERY, K. G., THE VISCOUNT OF ALAMEIN. *Memoirs.* Cleveland and New York: The World Publishing Company, 1958.

NOTHOMB, PIERRE, *Le roi Albert.* Louvain: Editions Rex, n.d.

PETRIE, CHARLES. *Monarchy in the 20th Century.* London: Andrew Dakers, Ltd., 1952.

PHOLIEN, JOSEPH. *Considération sur le testament politique du roi 25 janvier 1944.* Ixelles: Imprimerie et Publicité du Marais, 1944.

PIRENNE, HENRI. *Histoire de Belgique.* 6 vols. Bruxelles: H. Lamertin, 1909–1926.

RONSE, EDMUND. *Le procès de Léopold.* Gand: Het Volk, 1945.

SCHEPERS, ROBERT. *Lettre à un ami libéral (après le coup de force).* Bruxelles: Phare-Dimanche, n.d.

SIMON, A. CHANOINE. *Le parti catholique belge.* Bruxelles: La Renaissance du Livre, 1958.

SPIRO, HERBERT J. *Government by Constitution.* New York: Random House, 1959.

THOMPSON, DAVID. *Democracy in France.* New York: Oxford University Press, 1949.

TIRTIAUX, ALBERT. *La "trahison" du roi des Belges.* Paris: Albert Tirtiaux, 1941.

VANHAESENDONCK, EMILE. *Constitution belge, textes exacts de la constitution belge et de la loi provinciale.* Bruxelles: Imprimerie Emile Guyot, 1948.

VAN KALKEN, FRANS. *Histoire de Belgique.* Bruxelles: Office de Publicité, Anc. Etabliss. J. Lebègue et Cie., Editeurs, Société Coopérative, 1944.

——. *Entre deux guerres, esquisse de la vie politique en Belgique de 1918 à 1940.* Bruxelles: Office de Publicité, Anc. Etabliss. J. Lebègue et Cie., Editeurs, Société Coopérative, 1944.

VAN OVERSTRAETEN, GÉNÉRAL. *Albert I–Léopold III, vingt ans de politique militaire belge, 1920–1940.* Bruges: Desclée de Brouwer, 1946.

WILLIAMS, PHILIP. *Politics in Postwar France.* London: Longmans, Green and Co., 1954.

WODON, LOUIS. *Considération sur la séparation et la délégation des pouvoirs en droit public belge.* Bruxelles: Académie royale de Belgique, 1942.

WULLUS-RUDIGER, J. *Les origines internationales du drame belge de 1940.* Bruxelles: Editions Vanderlinden, 1950.

Newspapers

La Dernière Heure (Liberal).
Le Drapeau Rouge (Communist).
La Libre Belgique (Catholic conservative).
Le Peuple (Socialist).
Le Soir (Independent; however, on the royal question, anti-Leopold. The newspaper follows a policy of maintaining an open editorial column on page one which may be used as a forum for qualified contributors of any political complexion.)

Periodical Literature

"Après l'appel du roi," *Le Flambeau*, No. 2 (mars–avril, 1952), 97–100.

"Au delà de la question royale," *Les Cahiers socialistes* (juillet–août, 1945), pp. 40–43.

"The Belgian Crisis," *News from Belgium and the Belgian Congo,* V, No. 23 (July 21, 1945), 174–84.

"Consultation populaire et question royale. Point de vue et arguments du P.S.C.," *P.S.C. Bulletin d'Information* (janvier–février, 1950), pp. 1–22.

"Do Belgians Want Leopold's Return?" *Belgium* (August, 1945), pp. 260–73.

"Les grèves politiques à propos de la question royale," *C.S.C. Bulletin mensuel de la Confédération des Syndicats chrétiens en Belgique* (août–septembre, 1950), pp. 531–61.

"Où va le régime belge?" *Le Flambeau,* No. 5 (septembre–octobre, 1957), 577–95.

"Le pacte," *Journal des Tribunaux* (janvier 14, 1945), pp. 121–22.

"Point de vue national dans la question royale," *L'Actualité politique* (juillet, 1945), pp. 5–15.

"Le *Point* dans l'affaire royale," *L'Actualité politique* (septembre–octobre, 1945), pp. 3–56.

"La question royale et les 'Pages d'histoire' de M. Pierlot," *L'Actualité politique* (janvier–février, 1947), pp. 1–16.

ALEXANDRE, JEAN. "Géographie politique de la Belgique: Résultats de la consultation populaire du 12 mars 1950," *La Revue nouvelle* (avril 15, 1950), pp. 379–85.

BORREMANS, JEAN. "Comment mener la lutte contre Léopold III," *Communisme* (janvier, 1950), pp. 11–14.

DAWSON, CHRISTOPHER. "The Tradition of Christian Democracy," *The Month* (May, 1953), pp. 261–66.

DE LICHTERVELDE, LOUIS, LE COMTE. "La question royale," *La Revue Générale belge* (juillet, 1947), pp. 321–32.

———. "L'abdication du roi," *La Revue Générale belge* (juillet, 1951), pp. 345–77.

———. "La question royale," *La Revue Générale belge* (juin, 1946), pp. 137–42.

DE MAN, HENRI. "Winston Churchill et Léopold III," *Ecrits de Paris* (avril, 1949), pp. 55–61.

DENYS, R. "La question royale," *Les Cahiers socialistes* (juin, 1949), pp. 40–52.

DE VISSCHER, PAUL. "Le cabinet du roi," *Annales de droit et de sciences politiques,* X, No. 40–41, 167–88.

DIAMANT, ALFRED. "The Group Basis of Austrian Politics," *Journal of Central European Affairs,* XVIII, No. II (July, 1948).

ELEUTHÈRE. "La question royale," *Le Flambeau*, No. 1 (janvier–février, 1949), 82–84.

GANSHOF VAN DER MEERSCH, W. J. "Des rapports entre le chef de l'état et le gouvernement en droit constitutionnel belge," *Revue de droit international et de droit comparé* (Numéro spécial, 1950), pp. 181–97.

GATHORNE-HARDY, G. M. "The Democratic Monarchy," *International Affairs* (July, 1953), pp. 273–76.

GRÉGOIRE, HENRI, AND CARTON DE WIART, HENRI. "La consultation populaire," *Le Flambeau*, No. 6 (novembre–décembre, 1949), 608–14.

HEMELEERS, RÉGINALD. "La question royale," *La Revue nouvelle* (juillet, 1945), pp. 47–53.

HISLAIRE, RENÉ. "Léopold III," *Belgium* (août, 1945), pp. 258–60.

LADHARI, N. "L'abdication," *Revue internationale d'histoire politique et constitutionnelle* (octobre–décembre, 1953), pp. 329–37.

LESPES, M. "La question royale en Belgique," *Bulletin trimestriel de la Société de Législation comparée* (janvier–mars, 1948), pp. 28–48.

MATHIEU, OSSIAN. "La véritable affaire Léopold III," *Ecrits de Paris* (février, 1950), pp. 52–59.

MEMNON. "Le roi dans le gouvernement," *La Revue Générale belge* (mai, 1959), pp. 93–97.

MEUNIER, PHILIPPE. "La conscience nationale et le roi," *La Revue nouvelle* (janvier, 1948), pp. 25–35.

MOLS, ROGER. "Analyse de la consultation populaire," *La Revue Générale belge* (avril, 1950), pp. 841–52.

MOTZ, ROGER. "La question royale," *Le Flambeau*, No. 3 (mai–juin, 1948), 241–45.

REY, JEAN. "Au-dessus du problème royal," *Le Flambeau*, No. 3 (mai–juin, 1950), 243–48.

SCINTILLA. "Le drame Poulet-Capelle," *Le Flambeau*, No. 4 (juillet–août, 1949), 379–83.

TAEDA. "De la consultation populaire au message royal," *Le Flambeau*, No. 2 (mars–avril, 1950), 159–200.

———. "La crise belge et l'affaire royale," *Le Flambeau*, No. 4 (juillet–août, 1949), 345–78.

TEMMERMAN, J. A. "Constitutional Aspects of the Royal Question in Belgium," *Parliamentary Affairs* (Autumn, 1950), pp. 514–20.

TERFVE, JEAN. "La question royale," *Démocratie nouvelle* (janvier, 1950), pp. 41–44.

————. "La question royale," *Communisme* (décembre, 1949), pp. 26–30.

————. "La question royale," *Communisme* (mai, 1950), pp. 9–15.

TESTIS. "Le nouveau règne," *La Revue Générale belge* (août, 1951), pp. 505–10.

VAN ZEELAND, PAUL. "La monarchie constitutionnelle," *La Revue Générale belge* (octobre, 1947), pp. 801–9.

VAUTIER, MARCEL. "Droit constitutionnel. Lettres du roi. Article 82 de la constitution. Impossibilité de régner. Comment en déterminer la fin. Fin de la régence. Pouvoir des chambres. Principes applicables," *Revue de l'administration et du droit administratif,* LXXXVII (1945), 177–87.

VERCRUYSSE, MARCEL. "Comment résoudre la question royale," *La Revue nouvelle* (janvier, 1948), pp. 35–41.

WHIG. "La question royale," *Le Flambeau,* No. 4 (juillet–août, 1948), 353–64.

WODON, LOUIS. "Du recours pour excès de pouvoir devant la constitution belge," *Bulletin de l'Académie Royale de Belgique,* 3ᵉ Série, XXIV (décembre 5, 1938), 519–50.

————. "Sur le rôle du roi comme chef de l'état dans les cas de défaillances constitutionnelles," *Bulletin de l'Académie Royale de Belgique,* 5ᵉ Série, XXVII (1941), 207–19.

XXX. "Le Congrès national et l'inviolabilité du roi," *La Revue nouvelle* (mai, 1949), pp. 460–65.

INDEX

LEOPOLD III

AND THE BELGIAN ROYAL QUESTION

E. Ramón Arango

designer: Edward D. King

typesetter: Vail-Ballou Press, Inc.

typeface: Caledonia

printer: Vail-Ballou Press, Inc.

binder: Vail-Ballou Press, Inc.

cover material: Columbia Riverside

www.ingramcontent.com/pod-product-compliance
Lightning Source LLC
Chambersburg PA
CBHW021813270326
41932CB00007B/167